I JUST WANT YOU TO

KNOW MY NAME

By Johnny Burks

Acknowledgments

To my precious mother, Marie Burks Harmon. Mom, you saved me; I hope you know the love, respect and admiration I have for you and for the sacrifice you made in 1973 for that lost little eight-year-old boy.

To my father, Rayford Henry Burks. We did not always see eye to eye, but you were the smartest man I have ever known, and I know, in the end, in your own way, you loved me. Rest in eternal peace, Dad.

To my brother, your story, our story, is finally being told. I regret that time never allowed us to come to terms with our circumstances. Rest in peace.

To Tony Woodruff, Mr. Hartselle Football. I miss you terribly and I am proud to finally get this story to print and honor my word to you about the "real story" of the Fabulous Five. Rest in peace, my lifelong friend.

To my teammates and friends from the fall of 1982. We overcame so much! Especially to my best friends, Buddy, Lyn Long, Double Lip, Coconut Head, Chris 'Poochie' Keenum, Vic Coulter, Jay Halford, Katrina Clark, my teachers, coaches and classmates. Thank you for your love and encouragement.

To the members of the Fabulous Five: Buddy McDaniel, Tony Woodruff, Jonathan Anders, Eric Caldwell, and Fred Chatman. You all deserved better.

Pseudonyms

Marilyn Ridgeway's character is a pseudonym of a person who wishes to remain anonymous.

Anna Tate's character is anonymous and represents an individual working at Hartselle High School in the fall of 1982.

Big Red is a pseudonym for a childhood friend.

Prologue

When a man finds out he is going to be a father for the first time, an entire spectrum of emotions surface. That was the case for me when my wife first told me she was pregnant.

My wife, Alana, and I were teaching school in tenured positions and were building our first house. Life was great. Our child would come home to a beautiful, new nursery fit for a prince or princess. All of our friends were excited and baby showers were in the planning stages. I was on top of the world.

Toward the end of that summer, I cannot be certain of the date, my happiness and exhilaration about having a child suddenly changed to fear and despair. I awoke with a start ...a sliver of light under the door. Panic rose up in my throat and was choking the breath from my lungs.

Oh God! Not now! Terry! Where is Terry...wake up...wake up!

There her hateful face appeared, meanness and repugnance all balled up into one evil soul. I tried to scream, I could not make a sound!

Wake up, Terry! Wake up!

"Johnny, Johnny! It's a dream, it's just a dream," Alana screamed as she shook me from my sleep.

My wife was accustomed to the nightmares and my erratic, nocturnal behavior. She knew some of the stories, but I have always been hesitant to share the darkest memories of my upbringing with anyone. I wanted to be the perfect father and looked forward to the day

I would meet the first person that truly, from the very beginning, belonged to me. But in my mind, I could not help but wonder what type of father I would be to my own child. I was keenly aware that children from abusive backgrounds had a tendency toward being abusive as adults. In the silence and darkness of that lonely, frustrating night, I lay still in my bed and thought back to my childhood, back to that bedroom and my brother, back to the horrors of the years we spent in foster care, back to the nightmare that had been our youth.

Chapter 1

Bo, straight out of the movie *10*, was running toward me through the crisp sounds of ocean waves on a glistening tropical beach. Her sumptuous body seeping through a flesh-colored swimsuit, her braids dancing in the air had my hormones and anticipation rising.

Oh God, this is going to be good!

A shrill vibration interrupted the crashing of the waves, blurring Bo from my line of sight. The sound continued and I reluctantly opened one eye to see what was disturbing my romantic rendezvous.

No! Not now! Come back Bo, please come back!

I squeezed my eyes tight and begged her to return, but my fantasy had disappeared by the fourth ring. I grabbed the phone with agitation, knowing good and well what to expect.

"Hey, skruB! Get your ass out of bed," the voice on the other end demanded.

"Dang, Buddy. My alarm has not even gone off yet. Bo was almost there, man. Call me back later," I protested to my best friend.

"What are you talking about, dumbass? Get that ass up and get that game face on! The stands are gonna be full tonight," Buddy proclaimed.

Buddy McDaniel had become my closest friend since moving to Hartselle a couple of years earlier to live with his father who was a football and baseball coach at our school. With sculpted looks and a gift for gab, Buddy was one of the most popular guys at school. To the joy of those around him, and ballers, which included me, Buddy loved to chat-it-up about our upcoming opponents. Through clenched teeth, he passionately exhorted how guys wearing penny loafers and designer jeans had no chance against the badass Hartselle Tiger Machine. No matter the topic, Buddy found a way to ridicule the soon-to-be slayed opposition, and on this day it was to be Decatur High School.

"Hell, man, those Decatur Country Club pricks drink peachy-fruity wine coolers. Now you tell me, how the hell are they gonna compete with us?" he exalted.

Buddy and the rest of us were of the Urban Cowboy generation and wore cowboy boots and straight-legged Levi jeans. .38-Special's "Wild-eyed Southern Boys" was our weekend anthem as we poured beer down our throats as fast and continuously as possible. As high school seniors, our thoughts were consumed with three priorities: getting girls, drinking, and playing football; with the time and day of the week determining which priority took precedence. We were typical guys looking for a good time, and even though 'getting the girl' was a nightly obsession, hanging out and discussing our upcoming game was of equal importance. Most of the girls we dated understood this code of ethics and honored it. True Bama belles knew the four seasons of the year: spring training, summer workouts, regular season, and the playoffs. They understood our football hero crap like we understood their Debutante Ball and not wearing white between Labor Day and Easter. All were Laws of the South that were respected and never doubted or challenged.

Our weekend hangout was the local Sonic restaurant which was a typical burger joint, but with carhops instead of a drive-through window. Sonic boasted the slogan "get it in your car," and boy did we ever; not just food, but girls too. In our small little town the Sonic was the best thing going. It allowed us to eat a snack, love a girl, shotgun a beer, listen to tunes, and gossip with friends; all while never leaving the parking lot.

After realizing Buddy was seriously pumped for tonight's game, I gave up on Bo and rolled over; listening and grinning as Buddy rambled on with his usual semantics.

"All right, skruB. Run on to that sissy tub of yours and I'll catch up with you at school."

"Well thanks for the wake-up call," I said, sarcasm dripping from every word.

"Oh yeah! One more thing! The Senior Girls did us up right last night. Later, skruB," Buddy piped.

1 Hartselle High School Class of 1983

"Don't call me that," but before I could finish my complaint, Buddy was off to his next wake-up call. For some reason, I hated the name my friends had given me years earlier when some jerk realized my last name spelled backward was "skruB." What dipstick thinks of stuff like that?

Mobile, Alabama, 1965

She was young, still in her teens, and she was nervous with anxiety. She knew the pain would not last long and that all would be back to normal in a few moments. The burden would be over and she would gain her freedom once again. It had happened before and the choice was the same. The decision was easy to make as she had proven that she was too young and too irresponsible to raise a child. Immediately after birth, this child, like the other, would be placed into foster care. She was the mother I never met, and on February 14th, 1965 she gave me the name Johnny Roberts.

Time tells me that in the city of my youth, which was Mobile, Alabama, a heated conflict was taking place between the ideologies depicted by two completely different television shows. For many white citizens, Mobile was a town like *Mayberry*, a calm genteel place where you sat in rocking chairs on your front porch, eating homemade vanilla ice cream while listening to the Grand Ole Opry. It was an old, protective culture where boys were taught to be mannerly, and young ladies were their father's prized possessions and treated with the reverence of a brand new car. Yet on the evening news, blacks were watching Birmingham Police Chief, Bull Connor, and the city's police dogs attack innocent children. A hundred years had passed since the ending of the Civil War, and life for them had led to fire hoses, trained dogs, and church bombings. They were not of privileged lineage and were forced to exist in almost complete anonymity. They would be the first to tell you that Mobile was nothing like *The Andy Griffith Show*. They knew of a dark side to the town, one that was unsophisticated and secretive, a town segregated between the haves and have-nots.

Obviously, I was born a have-not; and when you are someone like me who was given up for adoption at birth, it's quite common to theorize about your existence. The story above is just a guess because I actually have no idea about how my life originated. I have no memories of my infancy, no letters, no photographs, no documents, and few recollections of being a toddler. The only memories I have of those early years center around one person: my older brother, Terry; Terry O'Neil Roberts.

Terry and I were never told who our parents were or if we had any other siblings. The fact that we were called brothers and always put together in foster homes made for even more questions about where we came from. Did we share the same parents? Did we have the same mother but different fathers, or possibly the same father but different mothers? Whatever the circumstances, Terry and I were connected to each other, and this made us brothers through and through.

Although the laws keeping the identities of birth parents and adopted children have eased over time, access to birth records was denied for many years. When your past is a secret, it is quite natural to speculate about your existence. I have always imagined numerous scenarios of how I came into this world. Considering the fact that I had an older brother, I first envisioned my biological parents dying in a car crash, and with no relatives able to provide for the two of us, we became wards of the state and were placed into the foster care system.

But as a product of the 1960s, I have also pondered the notion that my father may have been tragically killed in the Vietnam War. Then, realizing she did not have the financial resources necessary to care for Terry and me, my biological mother may have sought help and guidance from the welfare department. These are noble assumptions, but the ones that are probably the farthest from the truth. More than likely, my birth mother lived on the sleazier side of town and realized after my birth that she did not have the means nor time necessary to care for two infant children. In the 1960s, over twenty percent of unwed mothers placed children for adoption; but in Alabama, the heart of the "Bible Belt," the percentage was, in all probability, higher. Until the Civil Rights movement, the biggest question in Mobile was whether to declare the city of Spanish or French heritage. Questions regarding infidelity, abortion or adoption were scandalous thoughts that were discussed under the table or locked away in a departmental filing cabinet to be kept hidden until someone decided to seek the truth.

Terry and I bore almost no similarities in appearance. My brother was short and skinny with a slender, pale face that was flanked by long ears, gray eyes and topped with extremely blonde hair. On the other hand, I had darker skin, brown hair and blue eyes. About the only resemblance we shared were our short legs and small feet, so I sometimes accept the reality that we had different fathers. This leads me to the scenario of my existence that I speculate with the greatest reluctance; the possibility that neither of our fathers knew of our births.

I have sometimes tried to think of my birth like those depicted in television shows where family members and friends gather at a hospital delivery room to wait for the special moment when the adventure of life begins. Helium filled balloons, cigars and the jubilant smiles of brothers, sisters, grandparents and friends crowd the maternity room as a new family member is welcomed into the world. For some reason, I cannot imagine my birth showing any similarities.

I do not believe I was the center of attention as delighted faces argued about which side of the family I most closely resembled. I do not believe my bedroom or mailbox was decorated in the traditional color of blue. I do not believe I was caressed with the unconditional love and pride a parent feels from the birth of a child. To the contrary, I believe my birth offered a semblance of how aberrant life can be and is. I was born in a maternity room, void of the nurturing care motherhood should provide and left there to begin life alone.

Chapter 2

Football Friday, 7:30 a.m., 1982

Everyone who knew me understood my status as a night owl and cranky, resistant early riser. I usually began my day with a long, hot bath and many times nodded off to sleep in the soothing comfort of my brass, claw-footed tub. As a result, I would set my alarm clock on the sink and allow myself twenty minutes of relaxation before getting dressed for school.

"Johnny," my mother yelled, breaking my morning cat nap, "get the phone."

Dang, what now.

"Hello?" I asked.

"Hey, Johnny, I just wanted to call and tell you good luck, in case I didn't see you at school today. By the way, I'm running by Hardees. Can I bring you a biscuit and meet you in the parking lot before school?" the voice on the other end clattered before my mind finally registered the voice.

It was Marilyn Ridgeway, and in my mother's opinion, Marilyn was the sweetest and prettiest girl in our school. She was a petite, blue-eyed blonde with a perfect hourglass figure that drove our male hormones nuts. I had known her since junior high school, but she never seemed to notice me. To many of her classmates, myself included, she was aloof and spent most of her time chatting it up with older guys. Whether it was jealousy or envy, or perhaps the truth, Marilyn was the constant topic of school gossip. The latest talk was about a new nickname she had supposedly earned, "Peanut Butter."

"Peanut Butter?" I asked a friend.

"That's right," they giggled. "She spreads so easy!"

Marilyn had joined a pep squad called "The Senior Girls" and I was the player to whom she was assigned. Every week during the season, the girls doted over a senior football player by decorating their car or school locker with shoe polish, balloons, paper streamers, and the like. Looking inside, you might find candy, drinks, breakfast biscuits, or possibly a celebratory six-pack of beer for getting shit-faced after a game. It was 'special' treatment, and I was immensely excited knowing I was Marilyn's assignment.

"Well, can I grab something for you?" she asked.

"Nah, you don't have to do that. I'll be ok," I coolly replied. "I'll catch up with you at school."

"Promise?" she seemed to flirt.

Hmm, what to make of that?

"No doubt," I politely finished.

For most, school presented the same monotonous schedule of hurrying from one boring lecture to another. Football Fridays altered that routine by cutting classes a little shorter than normal for a mid-morning pep rally in the gymnasium. Hartselle was a town that nurtured football. In fact, the number of pigskin fathers who took time away from their work to attend the pep rally determined the significance of a game. For the first game against our arch-rivals from

Decatur, the gymnasium balcony was full. In the mix was an odd assortment of crazed football dads, former players, and addicted sports junkies who gathered every Friday to show their allegiance to Tiger football.

Year after year, men like Jim Corum, a booster club member who had not missed a Hartselle football game since 1966, dutifully stood with his faithful legion mulling through the same labyrinth of questions. Was this team good enough to beat the cocky snobs from Decatur? Could these players capture another regional championship? Would the dream of winning an elusive state championship finally be fulfilled? Was this the team that would prevail, or was it to be a third consecutive year of reaching the final championship game only to be spurned as the final seconds of opportunity faded to disappointment? In a few short hours, months of deliberation and prophecy would finally be put into action. Fantasies unfulfilled teased their obsessions, and each season the football fathers floated prayers to the heavens hoping their loyal devotion would be rewarded.

It was a new year, a new team, and a new dream, but the fanatic patrons of Tiger Football were a little unsettled heading into the fall of '82. During the previous two seasons, Hartselle opened with wins over Decatur and ended each campaign by playing for the state championship. Those teams were loaded with size, speed, and talent; but this year, the boosters had noticed a definite absence of college coaches stalking the practice field perimeter, and when the Decatur newspaper failed to mention a single Hartselle football player as a possible big-time recruit, a murmur of uncertainty and angst filtered through their debates.

As the marching band belted Notre Dame's "Victory March," my teammates and I marched single file into the raucous gymnasium. As a team, we were expected to show no emotion or acknowledgment to the crowd at any time, and while sitting in front of the zealous multitude, our "game face" was on full display. Following the cheerleader and band performances, the game captains were introduced and made their way to the podium for their brief get-fired-up speeches. Buddy was puffed up with pride as he strutted to the microphone along with seniors, Tony Woodruff and Chris Keenum.

My friend Tony was an average looking guy with an appetite for anything of the opposite sex. During science class, we joked about the girls running for cover whenever Tony walked into the room. He was the wildest and craziest person in our grade, and I often wondered how he ever made it out of high school alive. We referred to him as "Coconut Head" because of the thick, brown, coarse hair he combed straight down to his eyebrows. While on the football field, he was a cocky, boisterous lineman who loved to talk trash to his opponents across the line of scrimmage; and if there was ever a debate over who was the most devoted Hartselle football player of all time, I would have to nominate Coconut Head for that honor. Tony loved football, and he loved Hartselle football even more. Coconut Head was the life of every party and spent the first part of the school week recovering from his Friday and Saturday night hangovers. Tony was bright with a sharp intellect, but to his teachers, his nonchalant and lethargic approach to school made him appear uninspired and lazy.

Chris Keenum was affectionately referred to as "Poochie" because he resembled an English bulldog with his huge neck and broad shoulders. He was your typical Alabama male, born and bred, country to the core. Chris was a king in his own right, and his throne was in the field house, the third stall from the left. He viewed the most important part of his day as holding court and socializing with his teammates while on the shitter. Poochie was the team's outdoorsman whose exploits were legendary. As an example, on one particular occasion, he and Buddy returned to the Sonic drive-in from a frog giggin' trip with a black, rubber dinghy tied to the top of a car that had been christened with white athletic tape, "The Wet Dream." We all loved to gather around Poochie and listen to his tall tales while toasting his efforts with several bottles of beer. He had a lovable, sincere personality that made him the most popular guy on campus; but as a football player, he was a menacing, attacking machine with a nasty streak that we respected. He possessed the destructive attitude every coach desired, and his single mission was to inflict pain on anyone brave enough to cross the line of scrimmage and enter his domain.

After the fervor of the pep rally concluded, I found myself in economics class with the infamous David 'Dick' Townsend. Mr. Townsend was an older teacher who was counting down the days until he could retire to his fishing addiction. He was short and fat with a buzzed Sgt. Carter type haircut. He wore basically the same outfit every day: dark nylon slacks pulled up above his fat belly, a white shirt and weathered leather shoes. When Dick lectured, he would rock back and forth as he leaned on his podium. He chewed tobacco constantly, and it was such a disgusting visual when he would lean to his right and drop a long line of black spit into a brass spittoon. Those who had him later in the day got to experience a black ring circling his lips created by the tobacco juice he continuously drooled all day long. Rumors circulated that he kept the juice and used it as some sort of lure for fish. I still wonder if that was really true. I never understood why he detested me so, but one day he escorted me out of his class to the hallway where he grabbed my arm and told me that he and I had a serious personality conflict. I was shocked because I never remembered saying a single word to him or about him. Needless to say, I can still see that annoyed scowl etched upon his face.

As I sat post-pep rally listening to Dick, my eyes could not help but wander through a glass window into a school parking lot.

God, will this ever end?

I was totally oblivious to his ramblings when my daydreaming was interrupted by a knock on the classroom door. Turning to look, I saw an office-aide standing in the entrance.

"I'm sorry to interrupt Mr. Townsend, but Johnny Burks needs to report to the office," the aide stated.

With a disapproving glare, Dick turned to the brass spittoon and squirted a dark stream of goo, wiped his mouth and reluctantly consented.

"Your press is waiting, Burks. Better hurry," he sarcastically remarked.

With renewed excitement, I hustled outside, hoping I would be directed toward the football field house to watch a little game film with my coaches. Once I exited the classroom, I turned left, and to my surprise, my brother was at the other end of the hallway.

Chapter 3

My brother stood in white sneakers, gym shorts, and the remains of a summer tan. I had not seen him in months, which sent my heart racing as I quickly attempted to decipher the reason he would drive all the way from Florence, Alabama to see me.

Why is he here? Is something wrong?

Age had stopped his growth, and to my amazement, I realized I was significantly taller than he was. Our eyes never left each other as I approached. It was a definite sizing-up moment to determine the Alpha male.

"How ya doin', Johnny?" he asked.

"I'm alright," I responded.

The hallway was empty of all traffic as I turned and followed my brother's lead through the front door of the school.

"So, remind me who you're playing tonight?"

"Decatur," I countered.

"Wow, big game. Y'all ready?" he quizzed.

"Sure, we're ready."

"The star quarterback better be," he instructed.

I continued following him to a parking lot in front of our school. He turned to the right where he pointed to a blue Ford Mustang and asked, "How do you like my car?"

"Looks pretty cool," I smiled. "When did you get it?"

He responded by opening the driver's side door and instructing me to get inside. As we sat for a moment, I broke the silence and asked him why he was in Hartselle.

"I just wanted to ask a favor," he countered with a sly smile.

"Out of the blue, you drive from Florence to ask a favor? Crap, what do you need? A kidney?" I cackled.

"My brother, the comedian, ha. No, the reason I'm here is that I want you to help me do something."

"You know how Dad reacts anytime you're in town," I diverted. "He doesn't want me to have anything to do with you. If he finds out you're here, he's gonna get pissed."

"Well, Daddy Ray can kiss my ass. He has no control over me. I'm not his son anymore. This isn't about him. It's about you and me," he protested.

"Listen, Terrell, I've got to get back to class . . ."

But before I could finish, my brother angrily belted, "It ain't Terrell. My name is Brian, Brian Dale Smith."

"What? Wait a second?" I questioned. "I thought your name was Stoney? When did your name change?"

"When I got re-adopted, dumb ass!"

I looked away, irritated at his behavior, and happened to see my head football coach walking to his truck in the side rear view mirror of Terrell's car.

"Oh crap, there's Coach Woods," I hastily remarked. "I gotta go. If he sees me, he'll want to know what I'm doing out here."

"That's right, still the faithful brother. Anytime I need your help, you run away like a scalded dog."

"I don't run from anything, it's just that every time you show up something happens and I get tired of all the crap I have to deal with," I affirmed as I opened the door of his car.

Terrell was one of the best con-artists on earth, always trying to manipulate people and situations to his advantage. He had hung me out to dry on so many different occasions that I was automatically nervous and leery whenever he was around. Just before he was sent away to a special school for troubled youths, my parents found a stash of money, guns, knives and matches in a storage house in our yard. All hell broke loose, and staying true to his nature, he told them that I was a part of his miscreant schemes. He actually had them believing his story for a short period of time, and it took me years to regain some small portion of my parent's trust. I was not about to jeopardize that again, brother or no brother. Deep down I knew the best thing to do was walk away from this interruption and get back to Football Friday.

"Wait, wait, Johnny. Listen, listen," he asked as he stepped out of his car to follow me. "Look, I'm here because I want us to find our real parents."

"What?" I responded as I stopped and turned.

"Our birth parents— I want us to see if we can open our adoption records."

"Are you kidding, is this a joke?" I asked.

"It's no joke. We should know. We have every right to know. I've always wanted to know, haven't you?"

I stopped and stared into my brother's eyes. My mind was confused, it was suddenly as if the world was spinning faster and faster and all the air was being sucked out of my lungs. This beautiful day had instantly turned dark and ominous as I stood and contemplated his request. Why would he want to find our birth parents? What was his motivation? Why would he want to dredge up something I thought we had agreed to let go?

Mobile, Alabama, 1970

"Johnny, you better run. I'm going to take you to the jailhouse," Terry exclaimed as if he were traveling in a police car, sirens blaring.

He was riding a bicycle and I was on a rusty tricycle. Of course, since he was two years older, he was winning our childish battle of toy guns and high-speed chases. As I made the blistering engine sounds of my three-wheeled, imaginary motorcycle, desperately trying to elude Terry the Policeman, I felt his bicycle bearing down on me. The sounds of his pretend gun going *bang, bang, bang* now made the sound of a real-life crash as we violently collided. Upon impact, one of the handlebars of my tricycle punctured his eye. From that moment on, Terry had a glass eye; a glass eye that dripped tears twenty-four hours a day, a glass eye that never moved in any direction, a glass eye that would torment his self-esteem for the rest of his life. I never knew if the story was true, but it was the only version Terry ever spoke about, and I have always felt a sense of guilt because I know that eye was a heavy burden for him to carry.

After the accident, I remember a drive that, to a restless boy, seemed to last forever. Terry and I passed miles of green fields and tall trees that eventually led us to a red brick house that would become our new home. The house seemed huge to me as we pulled into the gravel drive, and I can recall my giddy anticipation about the large yard Terry and I would now have to play our many imaginary games. Large oak, pecan, and pine trees surrounded the country style home. We beamed with delight when a happy yellow dog sprang from the railed front porch to greet us. To the left of the home was a strawberry field with row after row of delicious fruit stretching as far as the eye could see. Sitting behind the house, and nestled in front of a thicket of woods, rested a dilapidated aged barn with a rain-rusted roof. A gentle breeze disturbed an old tire that hung from the limb of a branch, and to the right of the barn was a corroded swing set which appeared to have seen its days of children playing come and go. Our caseworker grabbed our hands and escorted us between a dated pick-up truck and silver sedan to the carport door where we stood in front of a lacquered wooden sign nailed just above the entrance that read "Welcome!"

From our first meeting— I am not sure what she did to give me this forlorn feeling— but I knew the instant our social worker pulled out of the driveway that I did not like this woman. She had a spiteful disposition and always spoke in an annoyed, terse tone. Her expressions lacked any hint of compassion, and she was quick to lash out if we failed to follow her instructions. She was average in height, big-boned, and a bit overweight. Her face was long with dark eyes, and her hair was dyed jet black. She rarely wore make-up, but her eyelids were painted with a tacky, shimmering purple color that magnified her feral demeanor. I remember her disgusting, calloused hands with fingernails sharp as a tiger's claws. Her breath reeked of a mixture of cigarettes and coffee, and the cheap gardenia scented perfume she wore did little to drown the noxious vapors that were released whenever she spoke. Her cologne was the type of overwhelming, drowning fragrance you smelled before the person wearing it entered the room. To this day, I still hate the smell of gardenias. I feel as though I am choking if I even get the slightest indication that a similar perfume or flower is present.

Her husband was never in the picture, much less the house very often. He was short, thin, and lanky with sandy brown hair and green eyes that sunk back in his head from hard work, sweat, and the hot Alabama sun. His complexion stayed reddish tan year-round and he smelled of Marlboros, whiskey, and Brut aftershave. From daylight until dark, he toiled in the strawberry fields. I remember watching him from my bedroom window at night stumble to the house after spending hours alone drinking in the barn.

As soon as we arrived to live with her, we were brought to the kitchen and told the rules of the house. I was a skittish child, timid and quiet, and first impressions would have led you to believe I was a mute. There was no warmth in anything she said, and I remember the emptiness I felt as she rambled through her diatribe. Being shy, I found it difficult to adjust to new environments and was thoroughly intimidated as we listened to her rant on and on about what we could and could not do. We were never allowed near their children and were constantly hawked to see if we were playing with anything she deemed untouchable. Our lives instantly became regimented and uninspiring. Each morning we were awakened by the sound of our bedroom door as it crashed against the wall, in the late afternoon we ate our standard meal of biscuits and syrup, and every night we were dismissed to the solitude of our room to wait for sleep.

My first encounter with her occurred on my birthday when she awoke me from my sleep and led me to the back carport door.

"You'll keep your mouth shut. Don't you dare say a word," she mumbled through a slow satisfied exhale of her cigarette.

She grabbed my hand while pushing the handle to a screen door. We stepped down the backdoor stoop to meet a well-dressed man standing in the carport. The gentleman leaned over and reached inside a paper bag where he pulled out a bag of M&M's.

"Happy Birthday, Johnny," he politely stated.

"Say thank you," she added.

I smiled a thank you and stood a little confused as I looked at the candy. He instructed me to enjoy them, so I quickly ripped into the candy while my foster mother talked with the visitor. Chocolate was something I rarely had the pleasure of tasting and just before I finished the pack, he patted me on the head and said, "Have a wonderful birthday, Johnny."

I turned and watched as he left the carport, backed his car out of the driveway and proceeded up the gravel road. Just as his car disappeared from view, my foster mother's demeanor changed. Jekyll instantly became Hyde as she snatched the precious candy from my hand. Pushing my right shoulder she marched me through the damp grass of the backyard toward a large flat rock that was embedded in the ground. Stumbling and struggling to keep up with her hurried pace, I could sense the anger with each shove to my shoulder.

We stopped at the rock and she turned me toward her face and said, "I don't want you to move an inch from this rock. You'll stay right here until I say otherwise, do you understand?"

I was befuddled and stood stock still as she walked back toward the house and vanished. I immediately began to shiver and attempted to acclimate myself to the cold, wet morning fog by sitting down and folding my legs across my body. Goosebumps sprouted from my arms and I began trembling in an involuntary attempt to stay warm. Staring at the house, I could see sunlight illuminating the roof shingles and knew it would not be long until rays of light replaced the cold, damp shade. As I shook, I tried to understand why I had been placed in such a predicament.

Quietly the sun crept above the distant tree-lined horizon bringing me much needed warmth, and a crystal blue sky replaced the moist early morning fog. In the distance, I could see two squirrels racing through a tree as they battled feverishly for the affection of a mate. I thought about how fun it would be to scurry for nuts or climb to the top of an expansive tree and watch the world pass by. I imagined myself in a position where I could spend my days moving through life with such joy and ease.

"I told you to stand, not sit! Get your ass up, you little shit!" she yelled from the carport.

Her voice made the hair on the back of my neck stand on end. The fear I had for her was way too big an emotion for such a young boy to feel, but I felt it. Instantly, I rose to her instruction, hoping she would not move any closer. I took a long, deep swallow when I saw her march ever so deliberately toward me.

Once in front of me, she spat, "I'm sick and tired of the shit you and your stupid ass brother leave. I'm not your damn maid, and I'm not going to clean up after y'all. Do you know how lucky you are to have a roof over your little shitty heads? Do you?"

I stood petrified, unable to make an audible sound.

"Why in the hell would that bastard brother of yours want to sleep in piss? I've told him to stop for the last time! I was not put on this earth to clean up his stinky messes! I've cleaned up all the piss I'm going to. Do you hear me? Your ass will stay on this rock all damn day! You're not going anywhere!" she ordered before stomping back to the house.

I stood and stood as the early morning sun ever so slowly drifted across the sky.

"Here boy, here boy," I pleaded to the meandering yellow dog that had soon become my only friend.

When Terry left for school, I spent my time alone with the only exception being the yellow dog. I do not remember his name, but I'm reminded that he was a boy because he hiked his leg to pee. He was scraggly in appearance with coarse thin hair, but he was young and energetic and his eyes expressed excitement. He loved to run and race and would yelp with an excited high pitched bark.

"You're such a good boy," I told him as my despair was temporarily pardoned.

My canine friend patiently played with me and nuzzled my hand for more devotion if my concentration wavered. But being a creature of habit he soon strayed toward the gravel road to continue his daily routine. No amount of pleading could regain his attention as he leisurely disappeared with an apologetic glance.

Minutes crept like hours until a growing impulse to pee consumed my thoughts. With each passing second my urge increased until I started tiptoeing in circles, hoping that in doing so I could chase my anxiety away. Just as I was ready to bolt to the woods, I heard the familiar sound of the screen door. Her casual approach to my hard rock prison gave me the hopeful impression that my tenure in solitary confinement was coming to an end.

"You look like a little Indian dancing in circles out here. What's your problem?" she demanded.

I grabbed my shorts and pleaded with her to go to the bathroom.

With an astonished look on her face she replied, "Pee, you've got to pee? Well, piss then," she ordered.

I quickly turned and took a step toward the house, but just before my foot landed for a second step, I felt a jolt in my shoulder that snatched me back to my original position.

"Where are you going?" she asked.

"To the bathroom," I responded, as my begging eyes confronted hers.

"You'll do the same as your brother. He pisses on his-self, you'll piss on yourself."

The thought of urinating on the rock and on myself never entered my mind. I was seeing my need to go to the bathroom as a chance to leave my prison, make my way back to my room, and hopefully find a morsel to eat. I stood mortified at the situation, squeezing with all my might. A hard smack of her hand across the top of my head plunged me to the ground. I laid on my side and looked up at the calloused expression on her face. I rubbed the top of my head as the pain and emotion evoked boisterous sobbing from deep inside me.

"Get your ass up, Johnny! Stand up. I'm not going anywhere until you do exactly as I say. I'm going to find a way to get y'all to understand that I'm not going to tolerate any more of your shit. You'll either do as I say, or I'm going to beat your little ass till it turns blue."

Turning away from me, she walked toward a thicket of pines and I immediately rose to my feet as I watched her break a few small branches from a seedling.

Yanking the needles from her switch, she returned to me and exclaimed, "You've got to the count of three. One! Two!"

There was nothing I could do once she grabbed my arm. Fear had replaced my urge. I pressed my free hand against my butt and closed my eyes hoping that by some magical miracle I would vanish.

"Three!"

Each blow felt like a million needles pummeling into my body. No amount of pleading or crying eased the pain as we danced in a circular slow motion. I collapsed to my knees when a final blow ended my agony, and she turned and walked back to the house. With apocalyptic intent, I rubbed the piercing sting of my freshly tattooed lines of red and blue. I lost control of my bladder through my tears, and for the first time in my life, I understood my brother's pain.

While Terry and I were growing up I never understood why he could not stop wetting the bed. I did not know that some children sleep so deeply that they never feel the urge to pee. I did not know it would be a problem my brother would grow out of given time. I did not know that punishing him for his mistake only made the problem worse. All I knew was that as long as we were together, Terry wet the bed. And I also knew that every time he did, there would be consequences.

Chapter 4

"This sounds ridiculous," I blasted.

"Look, we have the right to know who our real parents are," Terrell countered with an edge of contempt in his voice.

"Real parents? Get outta here! My parents live on Short Street. I'm not touching this. I want no part of it. Today, today of all days, you gotta bring this up."

"No, Johnny! Wait! Let's talk about this. Come on. You're not going to turn your back on me, are you?"

"Guys, is there a problem?" a voice interjected from the front steps of the school.

Terrell and I had been so involved in our conversation that we failed to see someone approaching from the Main Office.

"Johnny is everything okay?" Miss Tate asked as she approached the two of us.

Anna Tate was in her second year of teaching and was considered the hot teacher that all of the fellows lusted after. She knew the guys liked to flirt and seemed flattered by the attention, but still managed to remain professional. I had taken her Business class the previous school year and was able to eke out an A. Because of my experiences in class, I knew she liked me, so I could sense the concern in her eyes as she stood in front of us.

"We're fine, Miss Tate. Actually, we're through. We were just talking about a couple of things," I explained.

"Good. Then let's head back to class," she instructed.

Never thought I'd be glad to get back to a class.

With our conversation coming to an end, I told Terrell I'd see him later and walked with Miss Tate through the front entrance.

"Who was that?" she quizzed.

"That was my brother."

"So you've got a brother," she realized. "The two of you sounded like you were in a serious argument."

"That's the way it's always been between us," I finished and hastily darted away.

As expected, "Dickhead" greeted me with his usual contempt, ordering me to my seat. I meekly slithered into my desk and slumped back into my world outside the window, this time with thoughts of Terrell and our past.

Crap, do I have a brother anymore? Who is Brian Dale Smith? His name used to be Stoney. What just happened?

Football Friday, 2:30 p.m.

The sweet aroma of freshly mowed grass tickled my nostrils as I approached the field house for our final team meeting. I took a long, deep breath as I stopped to admire the beautiful landscape. In the

South, the best-kept lawns can be found between the outstretched arms of two optic-yellow goalposts.

Inside the field house, the locker room floor had been mopped clean, and sitting in front of the room, a large rectangular fan circulated a crisp scent of ammonia. Each player's wooden locker contained identical shoes, pants, and jerseys that were folded and neatly stacked. I walked to my locker and sat alone for a few moments, glowing with excitement as I thought of the opportunity that lay ahead. The locker I inherited had been used by the quarterbacks before me, signal callers who had signed scholarships to prestigious universities like Auburn and Houston. Because I had put in the extra hours working on my game, I was throwing the ball well and my assessment of the upcoming season varied drastically from the concerns of the football fathers. I did not share their apprehension. Instead, I was intoxicated with the anticipation of stepping into the limelight as starting quarterback and the possibility of attaining the celebrity status the fathers bestowed upon deserving individuals. A long year of restless sleep was over. I knew it was my time to shine.

Slowly, the quiet dressing room filled with a hormone-fueled blend of testosterone personalities, and first to enter was Lyn Long. Lyn possessed a carefree attitude, and his laugh was loud and contagious and overshadowed every conversation in a room. His face was dotted with freckles, and he had a huge grin filled with shiny white teeth that glistened against the backdrop of his light brown hair. He was the team prankster, the one who pushed the buttons that made people laugh; the one who lit a firecracker in the boy's bathroom, then spent a school-record 90 days in detention for his dastardly deed. Behind Lyn was his best friend and comrade-in-arms, Jonathan Anders; a guy more affectionately known as "Double Lip."

Being the typical cruel adolescents we sometimes were, several of us created the nickname for Jonathan by poking fun at a slight imperfection in his appearance; he had a fat upper lip! The name, of course, infuriated him. So naturally, it stuck. Lyn even went so far as to make up a jingle to the tune of "Double Mint Chewing Gum." Our jingle had only one verse: *What's the single most favorite double in the world? Double lip, Double lip, Double Lip!* So stupid, but so funny when you saw Jonathan's loathsome reactions. On a particular day in ninth grade, I discovered how much Jonathan hated the name. While he was sitting on a rounded top garbage can next to the door of our homeroom, I approached some friends serenading him with the jingle. Lyn, of course, was the maestro, and the chorus continued loudly until the homeroom bell sounded. I was standing next to him as everyone else walked away and I couldn't help but chuckle because the more he stewed, the redder his face became.

"What are you laughing at, you sum-bitch?" he snapped at me.

"Don't call me that," I responded, offended by the notion that he assumed I had something to do with the joke pointed in his direction.

"Well, what are you going to do about it, you sum-bitch?"

That's all it took. Right at that second, my fist popped that double lip, and an all-out brawl erupted in the hallway. Within moments after the first blows were thrown, a teacher stepped in between us and stopped the melee. Moments later, we were sitting outside the principal's office. Being the rocket scientists the two of us were, we concocted a "we were wrestling, not fighting" story in an attempt to keep our butts out of trouble. It didn't work. We got a three-day suspension instead.

"Hey, dude, let's groove tonight," Eric Caldwell instructed as he strolled by my locker.

Eric used one of the lockers to my right and was my go-to receiver. He was a tall, skinny black kid who rubbed way too much Jheri Curl in his hair. To give the girls the impression of a suave ladies' man, Eric liked to dress in his Sunday best. He walked with a cock-sure glide in the hallways and sometimes stopped to boogie to whatever song was dancing in his head. Whether it was after a big win or at one of our high school dances, Eric loved to be front and center leading the celebration. During our football practices, he enjoyed finding an unsuspecting player coasting through a play whom he could unleash a jaw-breaking tackle on, which he termed his "Kiss." The truth was known that Eric had long, nimble fingers, a great eye for the football, and of all the guys on our team, he had the best chance of playing big-time football.

"I need everybody's attention," our head coach sternly ordered as he stood in front of his office.

Don Woods was beginning his third season as head football coach at Hartselle, and had the fortune— or misfortune— of leading our team to two consecutive state championship games, each game ending in defeat. Coach Woods had the quickest temper and most volatile personality I have ever experienced. I first learned of his temperament years earlier when I was nine or ten. I was taking swimming lessons through the park and recreation department and he was the instructor. Every time I made a mistake he would grab my ear and twist it. Years later, he was my ninth-grade basketball coach and I got to witness his explosive disposition again. In the fourth quarter of a game, we were leading by one point, had possession of the ball, and less than five seconds on the scoreboard. After we inbounded the ball, he became enraged at a referee and received two technical fouls. Needless to say, we lost the lead and the game by four points. It was during that same season he was promoted to head football coach.

Coach Woods was a stocky man with muscled jaws and a trace of dark hair circling a shiny dome. He possessed a loud, intimidating voice that, if angered, would rattle your brain. Being a stickler for details with absolutely no tolerance for mistakes, practice never ended until he was certain every play had been perfected to his satisfaction. On one occasion he kept us on the practice field until there was no visible form of light and cursed at the top of his lungs because our receivers were not catching the ball to his desired consistency.

Coach enjoyed his position, he enjoyed the authority, he enjoyed the notoriety. He enjoyed everything about football except for one thing, losing. Coach Woods was not a good loser. In two years as head coach, he had already won twenty-four games, two region championships, and been awarded the Coach of the Year honor twice. But none of that mattered because of the two season-ending losses. Heading into the fall of 1982, he was pissed, *really* pissed, and he was ready to demonstrate his frustrations to all of us.

The frequency and intensity of his vociferous explosions were like a slow brewing summer hurricane. As the days pass, the energy grows; frenetically evolving into a swirling mass of destruction that lays everything in its path to waste. Such was Coach Woods' transformation, and by the day of the Decatur game, his metamorphosis was complete. To me, he appeared as the whirling, spiraling Looney Tunes character, the Tasmanian Devil, whose bombastic vortex gobbled up every piece of food within reach. Coach Woods' appetite was much different. Instead of devouring food, Coach Woods was a thunderous tornado of blistering screams and searing critiques that consumed confidence, loyalty and trust. I had already been on the receiving end of a couple of his outbursts, and was unaware of just how many more were yet to come; not just to me, but to other players and even coaches.

Our practices were pure 'Hell' and it was definitely survival of the fittest. Before practice, Coach Woods would step outside of his office and pin a bogus three-hour schedule to a corkboard. But a more accurate timetable would begin at two in the afternoon and finish sometime between six and seven o'clock at night. Puking was inevitable, and I remember a preseason scrimmage in which an offensive lineman began dry heaving while we stood in the huddle waiting for Coach Woods to call another play. Seeing the angst on the player's face, Coach begged and pleaded until the player finally exorcised the foul contents from his stomach. Moments later, as I walked to the line of scrimmage, I began gagging as the stench of the vomit circulated up my nostrils.

2 Coach Don Woods, 1982

"I talked with the weatherman today, and he told me it was gonna be a great night to play. As I said yesterday, Decatur's going to be a challenge. But it's one that we accept every year. When you leave here in a few minutes, I don't want you out somewhere grab-assing. Go home and get your minds right. This is not going to be a picnic, when you come back, you'd better have your butts ready to play," he concluded.

He sauntered slowly to the front of the room and wrote on a chalkboard *Be Back by 5*, and turned to scan the room before exiting to his office.

Chapter 5

Christmas, Mobile, AL

Although the city of my birth is not known for cold weather, sometimes a blast of arctic wind pushes its way through the southland. If Mother Nature is really in the mood, ever so often she will provide a dose of freezing precipitation and send an entire population of unsuspecting and ill-prepared victims into disarray. Such was the forecast for our first Christmas season with our foster parents.

Early one cold and blustery December morning, our foster mother entered our bedroom, still clad in her housecoat and slippers, and instructed us to go outside and wait in the carport. Terry and I drug our lifeless bodies from our bed, rubbed the sleep from our eyes, and faced the brisk wintry morning in our pajamas.

"Do you know who Santa Claus is?" she sullenly asked from behind the screen door.

"Yeah, we talked about him at school," Terry confidently responded.

"Who is he then?"

"He brings toys to you," Terry answered.

"Why?" she followed.

"For being good."

"What do you reckon he brought the two of you?" she questioned.

Neither of us replied as we stood cold and perplexed.

"Here's what he left for you," she exclaimed as she kicked the screen door open and walked down the steps to where we were standing.

From behind her back, she exposed two bundles of switches, each tied with a ribbon; one red and one blue.

"This is what two little bastards get," she exhaled while grabbing me by the arm and relentlessly swatting me with the switches.

"Y'all had better straighten up because I've called your social worker. It won't be long before they come to get you," she snarled while continuing to flog me with my gift from Santa Claus.

Later that evening she escorted us to the bedroom where we were instructed to sleep on the hardwood floor. She commanded that she was not allowing Terry to ruin her mattress and sheets. Over the following days, and in spite of her beatings, my brother continued to wet his underwear. At first, he was sensitive to the whippings, but over time and much to her chagrin, he became more immune. As the days slowly passed, an impending doom settled between the two of us. In my nightmares, the memories I have of those times always appear dark and drab in colors of black and gray. They are the only dreams that I ever have that do not appear in color.

"Wake up, she's coming," I blurted from my hardwood mattress, just before a thunderous bang reverberated through the house when the bedroom door struck a wall. Terry and I both jumped to our feet once her distinct scowl made clear her intentions.

"You little bastard, you've got to be retarded. That's the only way to explain it," she crowed.

With a couple of bounds, she jerked Terry from the wet floor and thrashed his legs with her palm.

"I want that piss cleaned right now! Get a rag and wipe every corner of this room," she demanded.

Seconds later, she returned and dropped a bucket of water over the pee and ordered us to scrub the floor. I followed her command and wiped the floor as deliberately as I could. Within a few minutes, the floor was clean and I picked up the bucket and walked to the bathroom, pouring the diluted contents down the bathtub drain.

"Why the hell did you do that?" she inquired from the doorway. "Why would I want piss in my tub?"

With a goaded sigh, she shoved me out of the way and began searching the cabinet underneath the sink, "You two little shits come here," she instructed.

Muttering in a crazed gibberish neither of us could decipher, she spun around, and like a blustery winter snowstorm, she commenced to whisk powdered soap throughout the lavatory. She yanked the shower curtain and threw it to the floor, continuing until Terry and I and every inch of the bathroom had been coated with the white powder.

Clenching tight to my arm, she snatched a dirty rag hanging from the faucet and pushed me to the bathtub. "Scrub this tub until it's clean. I want all of this piss out of my tub," she said. She then grabbed Terry and left the room.

I slowly filled the tub with water and began scrubbing the filth away. Moments later I could hear the yellow dog barking, and I stopped for a moment to have a look at the commotion. A half-smile stretched my lips as I watched the dog excitedly digging a hole.

"I'm gonna kill that son-of-a-bitch," a voice stated from behind me.

I turned to see my foster father anxiously watching the dog. I removed the smile from my face and went back to my morning chore.

"I'm through fucking with you," he mumbled while banging his ringed finger against the window.

He pulled a plug of tobacco from his shirt pocket and took a large bite of a corner piece. He rolled the tobacco between his gums and glared through the window while leaning over the commode. With an agitated spit he chimed, "You'd better run, you little shit," then wiped his lips and left the room.

Slowly I wiped and sanitized the floor and walls before walking to the kitchen and stating, "Ma'am, I'm hungry."

"You're hungry. Well if that bathroom isn't clean, I'm gonna whip your little ass. How about that? I've called and told them all about the two of you. Enuff's a damn nuff," she quipped.

She clambered from her seat at the kitchen table and approached me. Within an arm's distance, she took a last draw of her cigarette and thumped the butt into my face.

Fear is defined as an emotion of alarm caused by the expectation or realization of danger. For many, the privacy of a closed bedroom is a sanctuary, a safe haven that one feels a certain sense of protection, but for Terry and me the bedroom presented unexpected terror and isolation. Each night my brother and I used the lengthening shadows on the wall as our guide to bedtime. Watching the wall as if it was an hourglass, we both knew that when the long shadows disappeared, we were to spend the rest of the night in empty darkness. Terry fell asleep as soon as his eyes closed, but for me, rest did not present itself so easily. At night I struggled with sleep and lay stiff and silent watching the door. No matter how long it took, I would not let myself rest until all the lights were out and I felt that I was the only inhabitant left awake. Sometimes the door silently opened and streaks of blinding light silhouetted her presence as she stood at the entrance in an eerie silence. The aroma of cigarettes and perfume swirled through the room like a swarm of angry bees, and it was not until she stepped back into the hallway that I could finally relax, close my eyes and fall asleep. Many times, however, the door exploded from the hallway, and while living with her, nothing was more terrifying than hearing the spontaneous sound of our bedroom door thundering against the wall.

For some, when you resurrect memories that have been suppressed deep in your subconscious, you create a chain reaction. One memory triggers another, and then another, and the domino effect goes on and on until its hidden power is released. For years the secrets surrounding our abuse were locked away in my mind with the hope that time would eventually erase all recollections of her. Once my brother returned to me with his request, I realized some memories are not so easily forgotten. Terry had opened Pandora's Box, and painful moments of reckoning would be the price to pay for resurrecting a past so deeply buried.

Chapter 6

As part of our pre-game tradition, Buddy and I met in the school's main parking lot after the team meeting and drove to my house for a pre-game meal prepared by my mother. For the first game of the new season, my mom had cooked two giant hamburger steaks, which she had waiting for us alongside a steaming baked potato topped with gobs of melting butter.

"You boys ready?" she asked as we grabbed a seat at the kitchen table.

My mother, Marie, was a short woman with brownish, wavy hair. She was a crafty lady of fifty-four and bore a resemblance, if ever so slightly, to Carol Burnett. Mom had a green thumb that no one in the neighborhood could rival. She was also a noted card shark, and her game of choice was Bridge. But for me, she was the best cook in the country and never failed to have a warm supper ready for me to eat.

"Yes ma'am," Buddy eagerly offered.

"Do you think it will be close?" she reasoned.

"Heck no!" Buddy excitedly replied. "It'll be over by halftime, there's no way they can stay with us."

"Johnny, I need to talk to you!" my father hollered from the den.

I reluctantly set my fork down and walked to the den. At sixty years of age, my father was a man of average height and build, but easily distinguishable by dark, thick-rimmed eyeglasses and thinning gray hair combed straight back over his head. From our first meeting, I knew Ray Burks was a serious man who didn't mince words. He was a child of the Great Depression, who grew up in an atmosphere of few words and even fewer emotions. Dad was the only son of Henry and Daisy Burks' seven children, and in my grandfather's household, he was the "master" and everyone catered to his needs. Family matters were of little importance to him. The only thing he was interested in was a bottle of moonshine and money; his money. My grandfather was a taciturn, affectionless man whose aloofness prevented him from forming a relationship with anyone, including his only son.

The first time I met Henry Burks, he was sitting in a rocking chair on the front porch of his house. It was summer, and he was wearing a long-sleeve plaid shirt with faded overalls and a dingy brown fedora hat. When dad introduced me and Terrell as his sons, my grandfather just sat quietly staring at us. In all the times we visited him before he died, I never once recall him speaking to me. As time went by, a rift developed between him and my father due to his refusal to accept the two of us as family because we were not of his blood.

After I was adopted, the relationship I shared with my father quickly evolved into the same relationship he shared with his. Dad was not the type to tuck me into bed at night, nor was he the type to kneel beside me and lead our bedtime prayers. For special occasions, it was easier for him to convey affection in the form of a gift rather than the more complex expression of a hug and a kiss. It was commonplace for him to send birthday or anniversary cards simply signed "Ray." My father literally became the incarnation of Henry Burks, a man whose suspicious nature prevented him from trusting anyone, including his only son.

"Did your brother come to see you today?" he asked as I became cautiously aware that he was seeking straight answers. "Why was he here? What did he want? I've told you time and again to stay away from him," he iterated in a nervous, agitated voice.

Who told him Terrell was in town?

"He just came for a visit, that's all," I promised.

"Terrell never comes for just a visit. He's always got something up his sleeve," he protested.

"He just showed up out of the blue. I didn't know he was coming," I urged.

"There's nothing good about your brother. He's sorry, and if you don't stay away from him, you'll be just as sorry. Have you told him I don't want him around anymore?"

"Yes sir," I assured.

"Then why was he here, what did he want?" Dad growled, demanding explanations.

"Well, he showed me his car, and I think he wanted to wish me luck tonight."

"I don't believe a word you've said. Your brother's a liar and a thief, and if I catch you around him, you won't be playing football anymore. I've told the high school he does not have my permission to see you at any time."

There was nothing I could say, I simply sat silent, brooding over the fact that Terrell had gotten me into trouble once again. If I told my father what Terrell had asked earlier, he would immediately jump to the wrong conclusion like he always did. As I sat and listened to him ramble, part of me resented the fact that he was more worried about Terrell than my upcoming ballgame. I started to wonder if he would even attend the game because he showed no interest in anything I did, and he constantly bemoaned the notion that crowds made him nervous. Whether it was baseball, basketball, or football, my father always found something else to do. He and I didn't shoot baskets in the driveway or toss the ball in the yard. Most fathers exert a lot of nervous energy stressing over their child's athletic performances, but not mine. He couldn't have cared less. He did not possess a single athletic bone in his body and never understood the value of competition. I never had to worry about the pre-game pep talk or the post-game critique. For this special game, he offered no words of wisdom. He simply let the conversation end and walked away.

During the restless time before a game, Buddy and I relaxed upstairs with my hi-fi stereo. Every so often, some of our teammates would stop by, but the majority of the time we sat alone and listened to music until it was time for us to report to the field house. Whether it was a home or away game, before returning to school, we stopped by Tiger Stadium and jammed to our favorite 8-track song. In front of the holy ground, we psyched each other up by blasting our air guitars and singing at the top of our lungs .38 Special's "Hold on Loosely." The song struck a nerve with us and became our good luck tune. As the last remnants of southern rock, we held strong to the beautiful melody blaring from the band's guitars and lyrics. .38's music became so important to us that early one morning, Buddy and I drove thirty miles to Huntsville to be the first rockers through the gates to their concert that same night. I made a pledge to see them as often as possible in the years to come, and even though I've lost count, I know today that number is somewhere between forty and fifty.

3 Buddy McDaniel, 1982

Once we finished our air guitar karaoke, we jumped in our cars and drove to the field house. As I walked through the parking lot toward the entrance, Terrell suddenly appeared in the corner of my eye.

What now?

Sensing the tension, Terrell smoothed out a smile and submissively opened, "Sorry if I got you in any kind of trouble."

"Dad knows you're here and chewed my ass out. I didn't say anything, but he's sure you're up to something. I can't get into all of this. I've got stuff to do," I finished.

"Just a quick question," he followed.

"Yeah," I sarcastically groaned.

"Remember the box of stuff we brought with us from Mobile? Inside mine was a report card. Do you still have everything we packed?"

I stood puzzled trying to process his question, "I think so. You mean the yearbook and stuff?"

"I looked at mine and there was an address listed on it. I think there's one listed on yours," he explained.

Why does he want the address on my report card?

"So what's your point?" I asked impatiently.

With Terrell, there was always a secret motive in anything he did, and while standing in front of him, it hit me, "Do you think that address leads to her?"

"I was thinking we could find her," he answered with watery excitement in his eyes.

"Find her! Are you kiddin'?"

"Damn right I want to find her!" he demanded.

I took a long pause and began by reinforcing, "That's all in the past. First, it was birth parents. Now you want to find that crazy bitch?"

I turned from him to continue my walk to the fieldhouse.

"I'm just asking for help, that's all," he pleaded. "I don't want to do this by myself. Just do me this one last favor."

I stood stunned as I watched him walk away and thought to myself, *he's already been down there, the address on his report card did not lead to where he wanted to go.*

Mobile, Alabama, 1970

Like meek little puppies, we did as we were told and followed her to the bathroom where we stripped off our clothes and climbed into the tub. With an unsavory sigh, we positioned our naked backs against the cold porcelain.

"This is your bed from now on," she proclaimed.

True to her word, over the next few weeks we slept in the tub and were awakened in the mornings when my foster mother turned the faucet and drenched us with freezing water from the showerhead. Day after day, I vividly recall waking to the same water torture, and night after night I remember the struggle of trying to find some sense of comfort as I lay naked in my ceramic bed.

The bathroom offered nothing but silence and darkness. Sometimes to break the loneliness of our isolation, Terry would teach me what he learned earlier in the day at school. I slowly learned some of the alphabet, I could count to ten on my fingers, and on one particular day, he explained to me how different animals search and find food.

He explained, "Birds like to eat seeds, bees like to eat flowers, and . . ."

"What do little boys who piss in their pants eat?" she huffed before jolting from the doorway.

From the sound of her heels pounding the floor, we knew something was about to happen. The clanging of metal pots and pans indicated she was in the kitchen.

"I'll tell you what they eat," she barked with a lurch of her hand to Terry's hair. She pushed his head to the ground, and with screams of agony, he followed her down the hallway to a bowl that sat on the kitchen floor.

Forcing him to the ground she growled, "Eat!"

To my horror I could see dog excrement inside the bowl she was pushing his face toward.

"Eat it right now," she ordered, his head inching closer and closer.

"No, Terry, don't do it," I cried.

"Eat it!" she yelled, then turned to me and said, "Shut up, you're next!"

The disgusting smell caused my mouth to dry heave, and I could feel my stomach pumping its contents up my throat as I watched the vain attempts of my brother trying to release himself from this evil bitch. I turned and ran as fast as I could to the backdoor, leapt into the carport and sprinted to the strawberry pasture. Projectile vomit flew from my mouth with every scream that echoed from the house, and then as I fought to catch my breath, a large, dirt-crusted hand grabbed me by the shoulder and walked me to the barn.

Chapter 7

Football Fridays, 5 p.m., 1982

A rivalry is a lasting, intense competition between opposing forces who desire superiority, and no better description defines the relationship between Hartselle and its next-door neighbor, Decatur.

Founded in 1823, Decatur picturesquely rests on the shores of the Tennessee River in the heart of North Alabama. By the early 1980s, the city was experiencing a population boom associated with the rapidly developing space industry in nearby Huntsville. Within a ten year period, the city's population had erupted, and an increase in residents, new movie theaters, malls, and schools sprouted from the landscape, creating a large upscale metropolitan city. Expansive subdivisions were developed in every corner of the town, which created a brewing sentiment in Hartselle that Decatur was losing its southern twang as the influx of engineers and scientists from the rest of the country gobbled up real estate.

My hometown was a railroad community spawned in 1870 when George Hartsell and a group of business leaders decided to establish a city along a strategic location near the L & N Railway line. When a post office was established in 1873 an *e* was added to the end of Hartsell providing the city its historical name. Like many rural towns, the business district in Hartselle ran alongside the train tracks, with the core of the city surrounding a small depot station situated on aptly named Railroad Street. A small nucleus of families managed to forge a modest living operating several stores that dotted the downtown landscape, but the town never evolved into a large metropolis like Decatur.

Hartselle was a conservative town, with a community proud of its working-class roots; a place wanting to be free from an uppity, privileged class. The townsfolk scoffed at the radical evolution occurring in Decatur, and ultimately adopted the creed that 'it was best to work in Decatur, but better to live in Hartselle!' The city was a complete antithesis of its northern highfalutin neighbor. Like the Hatfields and McCoys, it was only natural for the schools and communities to become antagonistic toward each other.

There was an era in which Decatur had the best and most talented football team in the state of Alabama. In 1971, under the guidance of Hall of Fame coach, Earl Webb, the Red Raiders won the state championship, and in both 1976 and 1977, the school fell one game short of playing for two more state titles. Six miles south, Hartselle labored in the obscurity of Decatur's success, but after the '77 season, the wheels of fortune finally turned. Coach David "Bucky" Pitts had spent nearly ten years perfecting an option offense which would allow his smaller Tigers to finesse their larger opponents. Starting in 1978 his labors began paying off when his team won nine games, including a win over Decatur, and the following year produced an undefeated season and another victory over the Red Raiders. Reaping the accolades of his success and more money, Coach Pitts left for the head coaching position in Guntersville after the '79 season, leaving the door wide open for one of his assistants, Don Woods, to take the reins.

With its success, the Hartselle football program was slowly becoming known as the state of Alabama's team, because it crossed the boundaries between the Alabama and Auburn football programs. The team's uniforms were an exact copy of the University of Alabama, and the tiger mascot was the same as Auburn University. It was a win, win for everybody on Friday nights; crimson jerseys, or Tiger t-shirts, everything merged perfectly together.

With a string of four consecutive victories over Decatur, the fathers were now convinced the years of being second class citizens were over, and a new comforting sense of pride filtered through their ranks. Pigskin fortunes had been reversed and now the fathers could revel in the notion that football had brought their snotty rivals back to some sense of reality. Times had changed, and with the decade of the '80s creeping forward, Decatur was being forced to measure itself against its southern neighbors.

I inserted a couple of foam hip pads and a butt pad into my nylon girdle and then secured everything around my waste. I slid a couple of thigh pads and knee pads into my game pants and made my way to the taping room. As prevention, Coach Woods required specific players to get their ankles wrapped before practices and games. I had never turned my ankle and held that it was a waste of time and detested having to stand in line and wait for my turn on the taping table.

"Make sure to slow down during your reads. Don't get in a hurry," Coach Pouncey instructed as he methodically ran a roll of white athletic tape around my ankle.

"Yes sir," I eagerly replied.

Don Pouncey was hired as an assistant coach a couple of years earlier and quickly became one of the most respected teachers and coaches at our school. He was average in height, with what we called a squatty-body, meaning a small chest but big legs. Defining his square, plump face was a pointed nose and the beginning stages of a receding hairline. Coach was from the small southern Mississippi town of Enterprise, and I loved to hear him speak with his long slow country drawl. He was actually the first person I ever heard use the word "dad-burn-it."

Coach Pouncey was well versed whenever I needed instruction as a quarterback. I connected to his work ethic and tried to emulate the standards he set for his players. He spoke and presented himself with sincere honesty which kept me grounded if I ever got too pretentious. Our relationship was genuine, and I appreciated his criticism even if it was harsh. I knew his concerns were deeper than just the typical coach/player relationship. He cared about me not only as an athlete, but as a person, and when I made the transition to college football, he was the only coach that ever came to see me play. I don't think either of us knew how much we would lean on each other in the coming few weeks.

"Keep your head in the game," he asserted as I slithered off the wrapping table.

"I will, thanks Coach," I assured him as I left the room.

When I got to my locker I saw Tony motioning for me to come over to see him. I stepped over and leaned close as I sensed his need for secrecy.

"What'cha need?" I inquired.

With a smile, he whispered, "I've got a case of beer outside. Find me after we kick their asses tonight."

"Dang, you are hilarious," I stated with an approving smile.

"Who can you count on more than me?" he confidently positioned.

Tony's parents were divorced, with his father living in Russellville and his mother living a gadabout lifestyle in Hartselle. There never seemed to be any ropes placed on Tony's comings and goings, and his life followed an order of its own. Much of his day at school was spent socializing and fantasizing over the virginal freshmen girls. His biggest interest wasn't academics, but organizing our weekend parties—many of which took place at his home. Like a cool summer breeze, word of a shindig at Tony's house quickly trickled through the school. The coaches knew of his lust for partying, but he was a tough-as-nails player who was dependable in the clutch, so they appeared to be willing to overlook his antics off the field.

The hell-raisin' at Coconut Head's house was fabled and attracted kids of all ages and grades at our school. Tony wasn't into checking IDs, his concern was having enough booze to last through the evening. In his backyard was an all-purpose shed that was used for a multitude of nefarious activities. My personal favorite was *Quarters*, a game in which you bounced a coin, typically a quarter, into a shot glass fullof

4 Tony 'Coconut Head" Woodruff, 1982

beer and chose a person to drink it. My record for consecutive splashes was thirty-two and I punished many a victim on many a night. But for us, the most important activity for the shed occurred when one of the guys appeared to be rounding the bases.

With a subtle wink of the eye, we slipped away and left the 'luv shack' to the lucky Casanova.

Finishing my pre-game routine involved a trip to the toilet. For as long as I played, right before it was time to leave the dressing room, I had to make an infuriating dash to the toilet. For some it's fixing the hair, for others, it's touching up the lipstick, for me, it was the pisser. The frenzied pace of getting dressed and the anxiousness of kickoff seemed to send my nervous bladder into a panicked urge to purge. It was an irritating habit that I was never able to overcome, and to this day right before a significant event, I find my way to the pisser.

Finally, it was time for the short bus ride to Decatur. I stepped onto the stairwell and walked halfway back and sat next to a window. My seating companion was Buddy, who sat next to me with fidgeting knees bobbing up and down. I lowered the window by my seat to feel the warm August breeze as it circled its way through. The drive to Ogle Stadium would take about 30 minutes, enough time for me to lean my head back and close my eyes for some peace and quiet.

Mobile, Alabama, 1971

Wet, cold, and death. The beginning and the end of my final days with the 'evil bitch' can best be described with those three words. Wet was how I woke every morning when she turned the faucet on to rinse the pee from Terry's overnight release; cold was the porcelain as I lay resting my naked back against the confines of my ceramic bed, and death produced my last memory of my foster parents.

Near the end of our time with the family from Hell, our muted life in the bathroom was interrupted by the constant barking of the yellow dog. My foster father had tied him to a solitary pole that stood next to a bucket of water, and the yellow dog continually voiced his displeasure with the chain that inhibited his freedom. One evening as I lay in the tub, I heard a distant voice radiating from outside the window. I climbed out of the tub and stepped to the window to see my foster father leaning against the headlights of his pick-up truck. The yellow dog was excitedly bouncing high in the air with the anticipation of being released from his irritating confinement. But no matter how hard he tugged, the dog was unable to get close enough to show his appreciation to his captor. With a final swig, my foster father threw a bottle at the dog and removed a pistol from his pocket. With a slow calculated hand, the gun was raised and pointed, and with one shot my friend collapsed to the ground.

True to her words, within days, Terry and I were escorted out of her house and driven to another location.

Chapter 8

Football Fridays, 9 p.m., 1982

"That's what I'm talkin' 'bout, asshole!" Tony screamed at his opponents, eyes red with rage.

"Shut up, you'll get us a penalty," I instructed as I grabbed his jersey and drug him to the huddle.

With less than a minute to go in the 4th quarter, Decatur had taken the lead and we were down to our final opportunities to win the game. Two hours earlier the tone of the game was drastically different. With our opening drive, we drove the ball eighty yards and scored when I threw a pass to Eric as he streaked through the middle of the Decatur secondary. Minutes later at the Red Raider twenty-five yard line, Coconut Head pounced on a fumbled ball and our offense quickly reveled in a short touchdown run that pushed the lead to 13-0.

Those that know football will tell you that the three phases to winning games are offense, defense, and the kicking game. Within the first eight minutes of the game, we had won the first two phases, but in the blip of a moment, Decatur snatched the ensuing kickoff and roared through the middle of the field for a touchdown. *Hartselle 13, Decatur 7.*

There was a certain amount of swagger in our defensive huddle during the first half of the game. The unit had performed remarkably well, forcing turnovers on the Red Raiders four offensive possessions, while allowing the opponent to cross the fifty-yard line on just one occasion. With the ball at midfield and twelve seconds left in the half, the Decatur quarterback scampered for a short gain before Poochie moved in for the tackle with two seconds left on the clock.

During the ensuing timeout, I stood near the coaches as instructions were barked to the defense, "Listen here, they're not going to punt the ball, so we are going into our prevent defense. Do not let a single Decatur receiver get behind our secondary. We need to keep everybody in front of us, and we need to get some pressure on the quarterback. Does everyone understand?"

As Decatur approached the line of scrimmage for the last play of the half, the sentiment was that it would take a miracle for our opponents to score as a wobbly Hail Mary pass floated to the end zone. Nobody on our side of the field needed to see what happened, the roar across the field told the story, *Decatur 14, Hartselle 13*.

With the score 22 – 16, and under a minute to play, could Mary pay another visit? Decatur had just completed their only sustained drive of the game and had taken the lead in the waning moments of the fourth quarter. After receiving the ensuing kickoff, three quick plays had brought us across midfield and within reach of the end zone. With twenty seconds left in the game, Coach Woods sent in the play, '59 Dig' which was a drop-back pass where I looked for Eric who would be running a route underneath the Decatur safeties. From the line of scrimmage, I could see the Red Raider secondary was aligned fairly deep, which meant Eric should find an open gap between the linebackers and safeties. I took the ball from center and dropped five steps back into the pocket. As the play developed, I took a short step forward and delivered the ball to Eric who caught the pass at the thirty-five yard-line and pivoted toward the goal line. He raised his left hand

and pointed the direction he would take to a wall of blockers appearing in front of him. Eric slipped behind his human blockade and headed untouched toward the Decatur end zone. From his left, a would-be tackler slipped through the barricade at the twenty-yard line. Eric sensed the penetration and attempted to hurdle over the top of the defender. While airborne, the opponent's helmet clipped Eric's foot causing him to somersault to the ground at the fifteen-yard line. Instantly, the ball squirted out of his clutches, and a melee of bodies dove in unison fighting for the precious pigskin. The tale of two cities came to an abrupt end, *Decatur 22 - Hartselle 16.*

It was a long, slow ride as we sat vanquished on the bus trying to comprehend the events that unfolded. A numbness hit my body that made me feel void of any emotions. I just sat brooding over not possessing something that was so close, something we had worked so hard for, something we wanted so much.

Upon leaving the fieldhouse for the evening, I walked toward my car, longing to go home and sleep for days. While opening the door, the bright headlights of another car approached, blinding my vision for a moment. Slowly the driver's window rolled down revealing the prettiest smile I had ever seen.

"Johnny, I'm so sorry about tonight," Marilyn's sweet voice calmly expressed.

Suddenly I did not feel so depressed, whatever adrenalin was left in my system came roaring to the surface.

"I wish I knew what happened. We were so close," I meekly responded.

We continued to chat until we both realized the loss had changed our post-game plans. Instead of heading to Tony's for a quick visit and a celebratory toast, I now stood alone in the parking lot, talking with the bombshell of Hartselle High School. Marilyn told me that she and her friends were planning to spend the night together, but they all went their separate ways after the game. With neither of us having anything to do, I accepted her invitation and jumped into her car.

A typical Friday night in Hartselle meant trying to look cool and impress the classmates while cruising in your car around a six-mile oval along Highway 31. As if we were following perfect GPS coordinates, the drive began at the north end of town where the Sonic was located. Three miles to the south was the Dairy Queen, and in between the ellipse was Hardees on the east side and McDonald's on the west side. My classmates and I would spend an entire evening, hour after hour, driving in a pointless circle using the four restaurant parking lots as turning points. Every summer, groups of kids struggled to carve out a niche within the oval where they could congregate like flocks of birds of the same feather. In the fall of 1982, the Sonic became my classmate's turf, while most of the underclassmen hung out at McDonald's or Hardees. At the southern end of the circuit was Stonerville, the home of the flare-leg jean wearing, Dr. Pepper drinking 'potheads.'

After finishing a couple of loops through the strip, we decided to leave and head toward one of many local bootleggers. In the Fall of 1982, our county was dry; meaning there were no alcohol sales. To quench your thirst you either had to drive thirty miles to Madison County, which was wet, or you had to visit a bootlegger, which is what Marilyn and I did. Just to the north of the Sonic was Vaughn Bridge road, and after a couple of miles and a couple of secret turns, we'd arrive at the home of a friendly bootlegger. One dollar per beer was the price for him to reach into a rusted freezer and pull out delicious cans of Budweiser that were floating in ice water. Even though Bud Light had been introduced earlier in the year, we stuck to Budweiser. To us, Bud Light was sissy beer for the guys in Decatur to drink.

From the bootlegger, it was off to The Road which was a graveled pathway that led to a dilapidated farmhouse sitting in a large open pasture. Guarding the entrance to the property was a rusted metal gate and down a few feet further was a single tall oak tree where you could inconspicuously park your vehicle. Many times, my friends and I would stop there and get out of our cars and drink a few beers, laughing and partying on into the night. It was isolated and safe because you could see a car's headlights long before a vehicle got anywhere near.

I was getting a nice vibe from Marilyn as we slowly drove along the gravel, hoping not to make too much of a commotion. We parked and sat for a few moments sipping our drinks when I saw her cassette tape collection. Not knowing what I might find, I started skimming through her musical preferences.

"I'm listening to a lot of different things right now," she explained.

"I can tell. You've got some interesting stuff."

I wasn't surprised to find The Police or Michael Jackson, but what made my emotions lurch was seeing a .38 tape in the mix. I pulled the cassette from the box, and being the romantic asked her if she would play the song "Caught Up in You."

"You bet," she followed. "That's my favorite song."

Wow, I thought to myself. I had not realized it was possible for a girl to like my kind of rock 'n' roll. She wound the tape to the song and then selected play.

"Let's dance," she said.

"Uh, really?"

I had never danced to the song, all I had ever done was listen to it while playing my air guitar. I was panicking in the moment because I had always pictured myself as the strong, silent type, not the kind of guy who would dance in the middle of a road in the middle of the night. I mean, I had seen that kind of stuff in the movies, but my doing it in real life was another story.

"Come on," she ordered as she got out of the car.

Feeling trapped, I said to myself, "What the hell," and took a long swallow from my beer. With a tight squeeze, Marilyn grabbed my hands and we quickly caught the rhythm of the song. At first, I thought we were being silly, but then I began to enjoy myself. By the end of the song, there was no way I could wipe the smile from my face. We stopped dancing, and for a long moment, we looked into each other's eyes. I leaned forward, and to my delight, she leaned forward too. We embraced in a long, slow, wet kiss, a kiss in which I could sense the passion, a kiss I wanted to last forever. I held her hand and we walked out into the moonlight where we stood quietly enjoying the moment.

Mobile, Alabama, 1971

The most frustrating aspect of being placed in foster care is the constant moving. When it starts, the moving never seems to stop. Terry, always the chameleon, adjusted quickly to change and even seemed to enjoy it. He was the type of child who would run and launch himself right into the middle of a swimming pool, arms flailing in the air while giggling with excitement. That was not me. Before I stepped in, I would check the temperature and depth of the water, making sure all was safe. To someone cautious like me, change was a struggle and the biggest struggle was stepping into another home, another family, another school.

As a first-grader, I attended three different schools before arriving at Morningside Elementary. The school was a few quick turns from our new residence which was located at the back of a cul-de-sac, the home of Clyde and Ruby Webster. The Websters were devoted Pentecostals, and Clyde was the pastor of a small church across Mobile Bay in the town of Spanish Fort. His wife, Ruby, dressed in modest clothes and kept her hair tight to the top of her head. She wore horn-rimmed glasses that seemed to evoke a sense of wrinkled resentment in her forehead. She was older with a petite, plump stature and her lips were drawn tight, revealing a seriousness in her attitude. Her short, terse responses at our introduction displayed little warmth, but she did ask sincere questions about our welfare and care which led me to believe there was a compassionate side to her.

Through the months we lived with the Websters, Ruby became the first person I remember filling a void in my life of a female role model. Even though she was not overly affectionate, she did have a gentle side to her and looked after Terry and my needs as best she could. Over time, I somewhat came to understand the apparent look of emptiness in her eyes and in her expression. As a young mother, she had lost her first son, Jimmie, in a car accident in Texas. At 18 years of age, Jimmie was a skilled musician who toured with country stars, Hank Williams and Bob Helton. But while asleep in the backseat of a car, the prodigy was killed in March of 1947 when the vehicle was struck by a train.

Ruby's husband, Clyde, was average in height, weight, and looks. The only trait above average about him was his greased black hair. Combed back and slicked to perfection, his locks and sideburns generated the appearance of an Elvis wannabe. I remember standing in the mornings before school, watching him comb and smooth his hair in front of the lights of the medicine cabinet as if he were still a greaser of the 1950s. Away from the pulpit, he repossessed cars from those behind on their payments. My favorite memories of Clyde Webster were the times he came home thrilled with his skill in confiscating a car. Bounding through the front door, he would rush in, and Terry and I would eagerly listen as he described his deft maneuvers.

My stay with the Websters was itinerant. We moved often, and within a few months, we relocated to a house situated in one of the historical districts of Mobile. The two-story Craftsman style home rested on a corner lot near Woodcock Elementary School. The inside walls of the home were dark and water-stained, and each room reeked of the decaying scent of wood. The neighborhood was lined with hundreds of Southern live oak trees, with their gigantic canopies covering the sky and their enormous roots buckling through concrete sidewalks. It was in this area that I discovered the most fascinating structure I had ever seen, a creaky-crumbling outhouse. I had no idea that at one time people went outside to use the bathroom. I remember opening the door to the bizarre stench that seethed from the hole, wondering how anyone was ever able to survive the nauseating smell long enough to relieve themselves. I recall laughing as I watched Terry climb upon the seat and demonstrate the correct position. He then dared me to climb on for a ride, which I did. Fearing that one false move might hurl me to the bottom of the pit, I cautiously positioned myself over the seat. As I sat inside the plywood shack taking care of business, I could not help but wonder what happened when the well filled.

Chapter 9

Football Fridays, Emma Sansom, 1982

Following the Decatur loss, we faced county rival, Albert P. Brewer High School. Brewer was a relatively new school that opened a few years earlier and was struggling to make a name for itself in the annals of Alabama high school football. I finished the game with almost a hundred yards rushing and felt good about my performance in the 31-14 victory.

After the game, it was another glorious night spent cruising with Marilyn in her car. Unlike me, Marilyn had a cool car. I was hoping she wasn't becoming put off by the fact that she was always driving us around. Her car was a white Ford Mustang with what I considered the best feature of any car, a cassette player. Boy did I ever love riding around with her being the disc jockey. For me, I drove a green 1972 Buick Electra 225 that I inherited from my father on my sixteenth birthday. The 'Titanic', as it was christened by my friends, was a floating boat because it was big and roomy, I could seat ten friends comfortably. Unfortunately, the car soon became my albatross because it only got 10 miles to the gallon, so I was constantly running out of gas. For emergencies, I kept a plastic milk jug of gas in the trunk that I robbed from the lawnmower in our carport. I hated the car and was embarrassed to drive it because it looked like something an old silver-haired woman would own. Still, the Titanic provided me with a valuable piece of information: I knew a girl really liked me if she was not afraid to be seen riding around town in my shiny green pontoon.

Our upcoming opponent was to be Emma Sansom, and according to recruiting experts, the Rebels from Gadsden possessed size and speed and were quickly building a solid reputation as one of Alabama's future juggernauts. The team was loaded with talent, including one of the best receivers in the country. Adding a couple of good running backs and offensive linemen to the mix meant we were going to have our hands full the impending Friday night.

"Strong right, 22. And I want that defensive end to believe the running back is getting the ball," Coach Woods demanded as we neared the end of a grueling Wednesday scrimmage.

I nodded my head and delivered the play to the offense. The design was for me to fake the ball to a running back and force the defensive end to commit to tackling the runner. Once the end obligated himself to the tackle, I was to pull the ball and turn upfield and gain whatever yardage was available.

"Ready . . . Red 11 . . . Red 11," I inflicted behind the center, "Go!," I blasted just before receiving the snap.

The play developed perfectly once I faked the handoff. I pivoted and slipped between two tacklers before breaking into the open. The only defender standing between me and the goal line was a defensive back who was zeroing in on my path. Instead of angling away from his grasp, I turned and plowed shoulder first into his chest. As we lay on the ground, I acknowledged his tackle with an approving grin and dusted myself off and hustled back to the huddle.

"What the shit was that?" Coach Woods crossly asked.

"Sir," I responded shaken by his tone.

"That's the biggest bunch of horse shit I've ever seen. That's not the way that play is supposed to be executed. I'm tired of this shit; you're not running what I called. Before I called that play I told you I wanted that defensive end to commit to the back. Did he? Did he commit?"

"Yes sir . . . I think so."

"Well, he didn't! But you wouldn't know that, because you're out here freelancing. I'm sick and tired of you doing things your way. For three weeks you've let this team down, and I'm about through with you. This season isn't about Johnny Burks, and I'm going to make you understand that. Get your ass out of this huddle. I'm going to play a quarterback who will do what the hell I tell them."

I stood astonished as he stepped away and continued to berate my actions to the team. I turned from his presence and angrily took a couple of steps, then threw my helmet to the ground.

"What the hell are you doing?" Coach Woods roared. "Pick that damn helmet up," he furiously spatted as he jumped in front of me and grabbed my ears, one with each hand. "If you ever throw your helmet again, I'll kick your ass over that fence so fast it'll make your head spin! Don't you ever show any disrespect to me! This is what I'm talking about; you're not with this team," he screamed while twisting my ears with his hands.

The rest of the practice was a hazy fog of sensations, and I quickly went to see Buddy after practice.

"What did I do wrong on that play? I mean, I know I was wrong for slamming my helmet, but I thought I ran the play the same way I've always ran it?"

"You did, Johnny. Coach is an ass. He's taking his frustrations out on you, and me and everybody. He doesn't like us. Never has. Never will. Look at how he treated the guys before us. That's your proof. If 'you know who' would've been the quarterback on that play, he would have been nominating him for the Heisman Trophy."

Buddy and some of my teammates were convinced Coach Woods did not like our senior class. Whether it was in the locker room or out on the field, he constantly jibed us for losing every game when we were on the freshmen football team. To the opposite was the coddling of the class before us who could do no wrong. They were lavished with so much praise that it began sounding like a cacophony of butt-kissing. I remember when he was coach of our freshman basketball team, he began scrimmaging against us and even took to mocking our skills. There were rumors circling that if push came to shove, he would dump

5 Taking orders from Coach Woods

our class and opt to play the younger players. I left the field house feeling hurt and embarrassed, with a flood of emotions raging inside of me. I knew I had done what I was told. He had no right to criticize me, then to humiliate me by saying I was not a team player. I took great pride in being a teammate.

Chapter 10

The focal point of life with the Websters was the Sabbath. Some of my beliefs today were learned while sitting on a church pew listening to the good Reverend preach to his flock. Terry and I had one special outfit that we wore for church services, and each Sunday morning Ruby pressed our clothes, wet our hair tight to our heads, and marched us to the car. The drive from Mobile to the Reverend's church led us into the dark depths of Bankhead Tunnel and across the bay. The tunnel was built under the Mobile River in the early 1940s as a shortcut to reach the eastern shoreline. For me, it was fascinating submerging into the murky darkness of the concrete tube then listening to the echoes of passing cars as they zipped by. At the exit of the tunnel was a causeway that led seven miles to the city of Spanish Fort and the Reverend Webster's Pentecostal Holiness Church.

Sitting tall and tranquil, the white wooden church was nestled in front of several pine trees that provided a thick straw coating to a sandy dirt parking lot. A tall steeple towered above the dry, flaky, white paint of the front entrance to the church, and toward the rear was a second-floor addition that provided classrooms for Sunday school lessons. Inside the tired church, two-by-four benches dotted with hymnals and paper fans stretched across the width and length of the sanctuary. In front of the pulpit stood a thin podium lacquered in a shiny gloss where the good Reverend tended his flock.

I find it funny how people are such creatures of habit. Every Sunday, like clockwork, the congregation shuffled in at their same characteristic time and wandered to their personal seats along the pews. While sitting with Ruby, I swiveled my head from side to side trying to absorb everyone around me. There were always the faithful sitting in the congregation and those trying to become faithful. Sometimes I would try to locate the people that Reverend Clyde called the "unfortunate pretenders," those who, according to the Reverend, come and go unaffected by The Gospel. Those were the poor souls he was trying to guide to salvation.

Every church has its distinctive mix of characters, and the good Reverend's Pentecostal Church was no different. Each Sunday I sat near a thin, white-haired woman who wore the same pink floral dress. Every time she sat down, the dress climbed to her knees and exposed dark, tan pantyhose rolled down to the top of her calves. Throughout the entire service, she constantly gummed her toothless jaws. Her voice was coarse and her laugh was a raspy gurgle, and each time she spoke she sounded as if she had a pound of phlegm resting in her lungs.

For those attending the services, nothing was more entertaining than the Reverend's sermon. He began with a slow dissertation from the scriptures, his eyes glassy with excitement. To his delight, every so often a hand would raise and a shout of "Amen" or "Praise God" would indicate agreement with his message. The fervor of his sermon increased as the shouts of praise echoed from the audience, and the slam of his fist to the podium grew more intense with each wail of "Glory Be," or "Hallelujah!" The Reverend Clyde marched in circles around the pulpit, increasing the decibel level of his proclamation between each frantic gasp for air. His snowy cheeks flushed with blood, and his hair flew over his head as he whirled around the podium lambasting the sinners.

It was during his exhortation that gentle ladies enthused by The Word began speaking in tongues. The eloquence of the sermon became lost in a bizarre mixture of languages as parishioners spat their mutters one after another. The words were unintelligible and grew louder and more extreme as the audience filled themselves with The Holy Spirit. As Sundays flew by, I watched the good Reverend save a lot of souls, including my own.

At the end of summer, the Websters enrolled me in my fourth school, Saraland Elementary. Being a little standoffish, it was hard for me to make friends, but I did find comfort in the tight quarters of the classroom and associating with children of my age. I scored above grade level on all aptitude tests, even though there was no particular subject I enjoyed most. For me, school was an escape from the chaotic existence I had been living and provided the missing structure and order I desperately needed.

Once in school, it did not take long for me to figure out my location on the social ladder. Once your classmates observe you wearing the same clothes to school day after day, your position is quickly determined. The tell-all for me were the faded orange work boots I wore. While in school, you learn that the more athletic kids generally earn the most respect, and heavy leather shoes do not allow for the nimble moves needed for physical education class. A costly error in relay races will never win sympathy from your classmates, and also goes a long way in determining your popularity among your peers.

After school, Terry and I tended to meet at the front entrance where we waited for our ride home. One day late in the fall, I was a little alarmed when I arrived and Terry was nowhere to be found. I stood alone for a few moments until several loud voices from beside the school caught my attention. Curious like everyone else, I joined a group of kids running to investigate. By the corner of the building, I saw two boys fighting in the middle of a rowdy mass of spectators. I slowly walked toward the tightly packed crowd and dropped to my knees in hopes of seeing the ruckus. I almost peed in my pants when I saw a boy with orange work boots lying on his stomach, pinned to the ground. Terry's body language signaled his surrender as his opponent triumphantly rose for the frenzied crowd. As the mob of students dispersed, I walked closer to where he was lying. His face and clothes were a dirty mess and his eye had fallen from its socket.

"I didn't do anything to that boy, Johnny. I didn't do anything!" he cried.

I became angry as I listened to the desperate words of my brother. All of a sudden behind the school, rage flooded my mind. To me, his assaulter represented Terry and me being bashed into submission, and the kids that walked away reinforced the idea that no one cared. I think this is the moment in my life when I realized how isolated and alone we were. This was an epiphany, for me, in many ways. I could not have been more than seven, and at this moment I was realizing such evils as hatred and prejudice that many children do not realize until much later in life. After Terry cleaned his eye and placed it back into its socket, we quietly turned from the playground and slowly walked back to our insignificant existence.

Football Fridays, Emma Sansom, 1982

"Be honest with me, Coach, did the doctors say if I would ever play again?"

"It's kind of hard to tell right now, Johnny. They believe you'll spend several weeks in rehab and from there who knows," Coach Pouncey replied as I stood in the carport of my house.

Earlier in the morning, we had driven to the sports medicine clinic at Vanderbilt University to have my ankle examined. Throughout the drive, I held to the glimmer of hope that I might be able to get back into action. I was more than a little nervous on the way home because not much was said concerning the doctor's diagnosis and I was worried about my fate.

The night before, during our first possession against the Rebels of Emma Sansom, Tony blocked a would-be tackler that opened a hole in the opposing defense and allowed me to cut up-field for a long gain along our sideline. I planted my left foot in an attempt to make a final cut for the end zone but instead found myself in the grasp of two Rebel defenders. As our tangled bodies fell to the turf, I felt my right ankle tear.

Oh God, I think it's broke.

"I heard it pop, Coach. I heard it pop," I moaned to Coach Pouncey who knelt to check my foot.

Coach said nothing while untying my laces and stripping my cleat.

"It's broke, I know it's broke," I winced, terrified at the possibility that my senior season might be over.

"Press your foot against my hand," he instructed.

"It hurts. It's really sore and I can feel it swelling."

"Grab my shoulder and let's get you over to the sideline," he finished, tugging at my shoulder pads.

I wrapped my arm around his shoulder and gingerly hobbled to the bench. I knew he had dealt with plenty of injuries and felt I could trust his assessment as I watched him tend to my ankle.

"Ah, shoot, Johnny. I don't know what to tell you. I'd be surprised if it was broke, but I ain't sure. We'll take a look at it after the game and go from there," he concluded.

My jaunt along the sideline had given us a first down inside the ten-yard line and an opportunity to match Emma Sansom on the scoreboard. Within a couple of plays, we were in the end zone and tied the score at seven. For a short period of time, the stadium behind me appeared confidently calm and serene, but suddenly, almost abruptly, the secure tranquility of the cool September evening changed. The Rebels took control and stormed across both sides of the line of scrimmage, wreaking havoc and seemingly scoring at will. I stood helpless as I watched our opponents run to their locker room beneath the bleachers with jubilant whoops and hollers after thrashing us in every aspect of the game, 32-7.

"What did the doctors say?" my mother questioned from the back door.

I hesitated with my response as I watched Coach Pouncey back out of our driveway. I stood subdued, not knowing how to answer her question.

"Is anything broken?" she asked, her voice as upbeat as ever.

"No ma'am. They said my Achilles tendon was strained and that I'll spend a lot of time rehabbing at the field house," I said, lifting a homemade cinnamon roll from a cake dish on the kitchen table.

"When will you play again?"

"They didn't say," I replied.

"They did not say anything about how long this may take? Well, that is ridiculous to drive all the way to Nashville and you don't know anything more now than you did before you went."

Mom, of course, knew very little about sports or related injuries and, in actuality, was more frustrated with the possibility of dealing with my restless nature of not playing. She knew I would be moping around the house and would not be happy until I was back in action, and she was right!

Chapter 11

Mobile, 1972

As a small child the main artery of downtown Mobile, Government Boulevard, captivated my imagination. Enormous canopies of leaves giving shade to elegant mansions interspersed with a bustling urban scene created an exciting addictive atmosphere. Late in the fall of 1972, my brother and I found ourselves walking along the shadowed boulevard with the two most important people to ever come into our lives: our future parents, Ray and Marie Burks.

My parents grew up in the isolated town of Grant, Alabama. Nestled in the rural northeast corner of the state, the tiny farming community sits atop one of the last remnants of the Appalachian Mountain Range, Gunter's Mountain. To the consternation of the Confederate survivors of the Civil War, the United States Post Office established the settlement in 1887 and named the town after President Ulysses S. Grant. The town was small, quiet, and proud of its 'country heritage' as my father liked to say. Once during a trip to the town, Dad and I were forced to stop in the middle of the city's main street to let a herd of cattle cross the road.

As a youth, Dad worked at his father's sawmill, and it was not long before he learned to detest the grimy, filthy work involved in milling timber. He spent his free time raising hell with friends while roaming the back roads drinking sour mash whiskey and smoking cigarettes. At home, he lived with six bickering sisters with whom he could not form any type of emotional connection. Uninspired and listless, he knew it was only a matter of time before his drinking and recklessness would either land him in a stained pine box or inside the confines of a jail cell.

In 1940, at the age of seventeen, he decided to pursue a different path his family and community could not offer and quit school to join the Army. The military immediately seized upon his innate ability to work with gadgets and trained him for service as a radio operator. During World War II, he served valiantly through a lengthy tour of duty with General George Patton's Second Armored Division and was awarded a Bronze Star for dedication to duty during an engagement in Germany at the Battle of the Bulge. My father spoke little of his experiences in the war but did enjoy describing a time he shared a few jokes and some bourbon with General Patton.

Upon being discharged in 1945, he migrated back to Grant to reunite with his family and finish his senior year of high school. With a war hero's reputation and money in his pocket, he was quite an eligible bachelor for the young girls at the high school. He certainly enjoyed the attention he received as 'big man on campus,' and it was during that same year that one girl, in particular, caught his eye.

With chestnut-colored hair and a petite frame, Marie Hodgens wore bright clothes that matched her polite, vivacious personality. My mother's facial features bore an uncanny resemblance to mine: firm cheeks, a strong chin, and eyes that describe every thought, and it is still a joke between the two of us when people comment on how much we look alike.

My mother's family was close-knit, and their affection for one another was rooted in my Grandfather, Herman. Mom loved to describe his kind, gentle manner, and good-hearted nature. He was a preacher, handyman, and itinerant ventriloquist who incorporated his faith and humorist outlook into his vaudevillian act. Grandfather Herman spent hours perfecting his craft and became good enough to be invited to perform at local schools and theaters. While a child, mom's favorite treat was spending time watching her father practice a new routine with his mannequins, Margie and Winston.

I knew from the first time I met Myrtle Hodgens, my precious maternal grandmother, she was an angel. She had the softest, most angelic voice, and from our first meeting, she accepted my brother and me as her grandsons and loved us with unbridled devotion. She was of modest height, but extremely thin, weighing only eighty-six pounds when she died. Her hair was long and brown and was kept tight to her head in a bun at the nape of her neck. She was humble and unassuming and never wore anything other than modest linen dresses which she stitched by hand. Ma'am Maw, as I called her, was the consummate doting parent who took great satisfaction in pleasing those closest to her. She possessed a sagacious wit, and I never remember her saying anything that did not make sense. When Grandfather Herman passed away in 1969, she left her birthplace in Grant and moved to Hartselle to be near my mother, her only child.

The Hodgens were a perfect remedy for my father's aloofness. Instinctively, Grandfather Herman and Ma'am Maw took dad under their wings and became surrogate parents. Over time they became a sounding board for his many frustrations, and their thoughtful charming nature pulled dad out of his isolated shell. The Hodgens instilled the direction and motivation he needed to break the chains of his unhappy family life and ultimately inspired him to pursue a college education. Within a few short weeks, dad proposed and my parents were married the day after their high school graduation in the Hodgens' living room.

To allow returning veterans access to a college education, the government established the G. I. Bill of Rights in 1944. Dad used the opportunity and enrolled in pharmacy school at Howard College in Birmingham, which today is known as Samford University. After graduation, my father and a college friend pooled their resources and opened a pharmacy in Hartselle. The drugstore known as Gilchrist - Burks Pharmacy, became a huge success and allowed my parents to live an upscale lifestyle. Mom joined several social clubs and was even solicited to work for the Chamber of Commerce's beautification committee. But, for all the satisfaction money can bring, my parents were still not happy. Their attempts to have children resulted in several miscarriages, and it was the final conclusion of doctors that it would be

6 Dad at work at Gilchrist - Burks Pharmacy

dangerous for my mother to continue attempting to bear children. For a long period of time they gave up on their desires of having a family, but after conversations with friends, they became excited about the idea of adoption. Through several discussions, they realized the age for them to take care of infant children had passed and decided to contact the Department of Pensions and Security to inquire about the possibilities of adopting older children.

When I first met my parents they were staying at a local hotel where Terry and I had been driven. Based on their expressions and comments, my brother and I must have made quite an impression when we walked into the room with our new haircuts and snazzy clothes. Being a veteran of the Army, my father suggested we spend some time getting to know each other by touring the U. S. S. Alabama battleship, which sat near the city's port entrance. During World War II, the big ship with a crew of almost 2,500 sailors earned nine battle stars for service in the Pacific theatre of operations. Following the war, the ship was decommissioned and in 1964 it was towed to Mobile to serve as a memorial and historical museum. As a child, every time I saw the giant vessel and its massive steel guns pointing toward the vastness of the bay, I felt a sense of comfort in believing the ship was the protector of the city.

During our exploration of the ship's tight compartments, I was not walking fast enough and made an impetuous wrong turn. As I hurried from one porthole entrance to another, the labyrinth of the enormous vessel left me no clue to where I was going. The fearful thought of being lost, alone, and disappointing my newfound friends consumed me as I reluctantly sat down, lost, and not knowing what to do.

"Johnny, where are you?" my mother asked in her characteristic high-pitched voice, the voice that was soon to become my comfort and strength.

Rising to my feet as she neared, I saw a soothing smile on her face when she asked, "Did you lose us?" Her polite demeanor seemed to express itself at the most traumatic of times, and even today, her voice has a calming effect on me. My father, however, was quite the opposite. Never having patience, he expressed his concerns with exasperation.

"You trying to cause me to have a heart attack?" he exclaimed, "From now on you stay right by my side."

After our experience on the ship, my parents held me close to their sides, and together we watched the wonderful sky slowly turn from a magnificent crystal blue to spectacular lavender red. This was the first time in my life I can remember feeling important or special, and I basked in the attention my soon-to-be parents were providing.

Finally, after we had driven all around the downtown area, Dad suggested we stop at the hotel for a bite to eat and an overnight stay. Once we arrived at our rooms, my parents told us to get ready for bed as quickly as possible because they had something they wanted to discuss.

"Come in, boys," dad instructed from the doorway that connected our rooms.

His eyes were serious and my first reaction was that we had done something wrong— shades of the past—but my mother came and sat between us and affectionately wrapped her arms over our shoulders. Dad sat on the adjacent bed and rubbed a serious hand across the floral bedspread. He looked at Terry and me and began speaking in slow, deliberate statements.

"Johnny, Terry— Marie and I have been hearing a lot about you two the past few months. We were sent pictures and had people come into our home to see if you would like our house. We have always wanted children, but certain things have not worked in our favor. What if we took you away from Mobile and brought you to our home?" my father politely asked.

Mom squeezed us as the words that were spoken took on somewhat of a surrealistic quality. At such a passionate, earthshaking moment in the lives of two boys, all we could muster up to say with almost an embarrassed tone was, "Yeah, sure."

Dad continued by saying, "We want you to stay and live with us and become our sons, Johnny and Terry Burks."

"Burks?" Terry asked.

"Yes. If you come to live with us, your names will change," Dad explained.

"What about our first names?" Terry asked, "will they change too?"

"You don't have to change your first name unless you want to," Dad replied.

Looking toward me, my brother responded, "I think it would be neat to have a new first name."

Perplexed, my mother asked, "What's wrong with Terry?"

"I don't know, I just like the name Terrell," my brother responded.

"Terrell? I don't know if I've ever heard the name Terrell," Dad countered.

"If you're going to change both your first name and your last name, you might as well change your middle name too," my mother interjected. "What if each one of you took a part of Ray's name?"

My father's name was Rayford Henry Burks, or Ray, as everyone called him, and mom thought it would be proper if we incorporated his name into ours.

"How about Terrell Henry Burks and Johnny Ray Burks?" Mother asked.

Without any hesitation, Terry responded, "Can I have Ray?"

"I don't guess it really matters," mom concluded.

7 When my parents were considering adopting me, they were sent a file and this picture.

Our short deliberation of names finally ended with my brother choosing Terrell Ray Burks, and me agreeing to, John Henry Burks. That was the day Johnny Roberts died and Johnny Burks was born.

Football Fridays, Austin, 1982

On the following Monday at school, Buddy approached me in the hallway and pulled me to the side.

"You're not going to believe what Coach Woods did," he exclaimed in a harried pitch. "That asshole kicked me off the team!"

"What? You've got to be kidding. Why would he do that?" I mused.

"He thinks I was out drinking Friday night after the game. I told him I wasn't, but he didn't believe me. Hell, Johnny, I went on a date with Katrina, and she wouldn't let me drink," he griped, his teeth clenched tight.

Buddy and my friend Katrina Clark were both on the rebound from soured relationships. They were polar opposites and quite possibly landed together as a kind of reassurance that they were still desirable seniors. Katrina was a cheerleader, well-known teetotaler, and was one of my closest confidants. We had nothing in common, and there was no attraction between us, but for some unknown reason, we clicked. She had starry blue eyes and shiny, black hair that was hot rolled to perfection. In and out of school, Katrina's passion was fashion and she fancied herself as a burgeoning diva and dressed in a meticulous blend of designer clothes. Her second obsession was gossip, and she had the scoop on everything and everybody.

Katrina was the one person who could see through my cavalier, somewhat macho exterior. She knew I was much more genteel than I wanted to show and delighted in finding ways to expose me as a fraud.

If we were walking toward a doorway, she would stop and wait with a sheepish grin until I opened the door. Sometimes, in the library, she would stand until I pulled a chair out for her, and during one Christmas season she made me climb on Santa's knee and have my picture taken with her. Katrina was polished in southern culture and indoctrinated in the art of proper romance. She envisioned me as being refined and expected me to treat girls with a certain amount of dignity that was not found between the walls of the football lockerroom.

Buddy sneered while jetting an evil glare down the hallway, "Katrina and I cruised around for a while before I dropped her off, and went on my way. 'Ole butt-lick kicked Tony, Eric, Fred, and Double Lip off the team too."

"Wait a second," I responded, "Why did they get kicked off the team?"

"After the game, they rode around with some of the guys probably stewing over the butt-whipping we took." He then braced the heel of a shoe against a locker and continued, "I told him I had not been drinking, but he didn't believe me. Then he asked where I had been, so I told him about Katrina and that around 12:30 I got a call from Tony who said they needed a ride home. So I told him I picked them up and drove everyone home. That was it."

After an uneasy sigh, I asked, "So what's the big deal?"

"I don't know, but he kicked us off the team for breaking curfew."

"Curfew!" I coughed, "What curfew? We've never had a curfew either before or after a game."

"No shit," Buddy agreed. "He said we stayed out past curfew and that we were suspended."

"I don't remember him saying we had a curfew after the game," I countered.

"He didn't. I talked with my dad, and he thinks Coach was after me. He couldn't prove I was drinking, so he creates the curfew crap. Because I mentioned Tony and everyone else, he suspended them too."

"What are you going to do?" I questioned.

Buddy stood tall and scanned the hallway before leaning closer to me, "Why did he call me in, I mean just out of the blue? That's what I can't figure out. I'm telling you, there's more to the story."

"But I mean seriously, what are you going to do?" I asked.

"There's nothing I can do. Dad won't let me quit, so I'm stuck. Shit for brains has thrown us under the bus," Buddy reasoned. "It's just like we've all been saying, he doesn't care about me or you or any of us."

That same afternoon, as Poochie and the rest of the guys prepped for practice, I soaked my ankle in an ice bucket in the film room and thought of Buddy, Tony, and the others. Coach Woods would not allow them to attend practice, instead, they were sent to after school detention in the library.

"What the hell's going on in here," Coach Woods suddenly piped from the doorway to the film room. "Why in the hell is everyone so damn happy?" he asked. "We just got our asses kicked, and on Monday we've got players tossing ice at each other. This is bullshit, I can't believe what I'm seeing," he snarled, with the opinion that it was heresy for anyone to be happy and joyous after being thumped so rudely the week before.

A wave of silence seeped through the room as his irritated voice instructed, "Everybody get their asses in the locker room!"

Quietly we walked to our lockers, knowing the shockwave of a sonic boom was about to shatter our eardrums.

"Let me tell you something. I've been here since 1969, and I've never seen such a group of lousy, shitty players. You make me sick," he growled.

"You don't get it. You're letting me, yourselves, your family, and this community down. It makes my blood boil to think of the wasted talent sitting in here. You have no work ethic, no desire, and let me tell you something, this room is for football players, not clowns, drunks or dope heads," he continued as the veins on his shiny dome pooled with blood.

"I'm not going to let any of you ruin this program. I've already suspended five guys for not giving a shit about this season. Hanging out till all hours in the morning was more important than this team. Lack of dedication and commitment is what all of you lack," he screamed.

Coach Woods continued his rant and described us as a bunch of gutless wonders, then blatantly challenged one player to step outside and fight, and for a moment his challenge was almost accepted.

As I continued to listen to the utter bull spewing out of his mouth, I thought about the number of times I defended his antics to my teammates and seriously began to question whether or not they were right. There were occasions when I thought I understood him, even felt sorry for him. But those occurrences were becoming fewer and farther apart. In reality, his ego was monstrously large and his patience and volatile emotions rested on his sleeve like a smoldering fire waiting to rage. Surrounding him was an egomaniacal shell that prevented anyone from connecting with him on a friendly basis. Sometimes he lauded players with superlatives and was boisterous and fun to be around, but there was another side to his personality that was spiteful and harsh that made you seethe with disdain.

After completing his thirty-minute barrage, he ordered us to get out of the dressing room as quickly as possible because practice was canceled.

The dressing room quickly cleared until Poochie and I were the only players left, "What'll we do, skruB?" he asked.

"I don't know," I replied, shrugging my shoulders.

"You're hurt. Buddy, Tony, Double Lip, Fred, and Eric are suspended. And, Steve Barnett says his thigh hurts and he can't run. That's seven starters, and there's a rumor he's going to suspend someone else. And then, to top all of that off, we don't practice today."

I squinted my eyes to a serious face and said, "I don't know, Poochie, everything we do is wrong or not good enough. It's getting to where it's not even fun anymore. I mean we've worked our butts off for years, we've done everything asked of us. He just keeps sucking the life out of this season."

Poochie was the one guy on the team everyone respected. He had a "take no prisoner" approach, and came to practice every day bouncing with excited energy. His reputation as a fighter and badass was not given to him, it was earned during spring drills of our freshman year. Toward the end of practice one afternoon, Coach Woods called the team together for a one-on-one blocking drill known as Oklahoma. With all eyes watching, Poochie was ordered to step in and block one of the upperclassmen. He enthusiastically knelt in his stance and when Coach blew his whistle, he attacked his much larger foe like a rabid dog. To everyone's amazement and enjoyment, he drove his challenger backward and into the ground continuing his all-out assault, and kept driving his feet until his victim's face was buried to submission.

Everyone who watched Poochie marveled at his dogged determination and relentless spirit. In the weight room, he was the strongest guy on the team and bench pressed over three hundred pounds. His never-say-quit attitude allowed him to push his body to the limit, and not even summer surgery for a hernia kept him off the field during our senior season. Winning was important to Poochie, and he was determined to win the right way.

"I don't wanna go out this way, Johnny," he complained.

8 Tony (facing) with Poochie and Coach Joe Weaver

"None of us do. Right now you've got to take the lead and hold everyone together," I finished.

I stepped into my car, turned the radio on and thought about the quick manner in which the season had evolved. Weeks earlier, the buzz in the barbershop centered around a third straight trip to the playoffs. Expectations were high. Now we were losers, underachievers, and according to Coach Woods, the worst players to pass through the program in decades.

Chapter 12

It was a couple of weeks from Homecoming and Marilyn and I had blossomed into what I hoped was boyfriend and girlfriend. Late on Sunday afternoons, we would meet near the Civic Center and spend the afternoon walking along trails weaving through Sparkman Park. Even though we were classmates, I had never been afforded a real opportunity to know her. At school, we floated around the same social circles, but for some reason, we never found time to talk to each other. As we approached a small creek snaking its way through the undergrowth, I was struggling with an important question I had been wanting to ask her, but my nerves kept getting in the way.

"Alright Johnny, what's going on?" she asked.

"What do you mean," I responded.

"I can tell there's something going on in that head of yours. So, what is it?" she followed.

We stopped and she grabbed my hand and smiled.

"Well," I stammered, "Well."

"Well, what? What is it?" she opined.

"Uh, will you go to Homecoming with me?" I relented.

I managed a slight cough and an awkward smile when our eyes locked. My heart raced with adrenalin once she acknowledged my embarrassment with a soft, sensuous smile. Suddenly I was teetering between shameless desires and desperation. I instantly knew there was no way I could camouflage my expressions.

"I was wondering if you were ever going to ask," she remarked. "We're going to have the best Homecoming ever!"

I was so happy and reached my arms around her with earnest affection as we embraced.

Football Fridays, Austin, 1982

The Black Bears scored again late in the fourth quarter to make the final score 26-7. Our record dropped to 1-3, and as a team, we were at rock bottom with seemingly little chance of salvaging the season. I stood along the sideline and cheered everyone's efforts, but it was a hopeless cause. After the game, I followed my teammates onto the bus and found a seat near the front.

"Get up, Burks. The walking wounded don't get a seat," Coach Woods ordered.

"Sir," I responded puzzled.

"Get your ass up and give that seat to someone in a uniform," he demanded.

The walking wounded? Man, was I pissed. And, as if it could not get any worse, I stood up and gave my seat to someone just like me, someone who had not stepped onto the field and played a single down.

My embarrassment following the Austin game paled in comparison to 'the Fabulous Five,' which was the name Coach Woods coined for

Buddy, Tony, and the rest of the curfew breakers. To add insult to injury before the game, Coach Woods told the five that they could not ride with the team to the game nor stand on the sidelines during the game, then taunted them by saying, "And, if you want to go to the game, buy a ticket."

And, that is just what they did. Like Hester Prynne and her scarlet letter, 'the Fabulous Five' sat in the bleachers that Friday night for every scornful eye to see. However, those eyes had been blinded to the truth. The entire incident of Buddy drinking and breaking curfew was based on a lie. According to revelations that were quickly discovered, after his date with Katrina, Buddy was invited to another girl's house. That girl's former boyfriend along with a couple of other guys, all teammates of ours from the previous season, also appeared at the house and were shocked to see Buddy. Whether it was revenge, jealousy, or some other motive, the fact that former teammates concocted the drinking story and shared it with Coach Woods was a bitter pill for Buddy to swallow.

In the aftermath, Coach Woods dropped the drinking accusation, but held firm to the curfew violation which was even more egregious because there was absolutely no team curfew. I cannot remember a time Coach Woods, or any coach, called or stopped by my house to see if I was home. Curfews were dictated and enforced by parents, not coaches. Coconut Head, Double Lip, Eric, and Fred did nothing wrong but were collateral damage when someone who was judge, jury, and executioner refused to listen and own up to the truth.

The notion that Coach Woods would go out of his way to suspend 'the Fabulous Five' was made even worse when the fallacious story was released to the local newspapers prior to the game. Printed in black ink on white paper, five eighteen-year-old boys were further humiliated by

Coach Woods when the news was exposed to the public. Could not a few wind sprints have been an option for breaking a curfew rule that did not exist? Coach Woods' actions seemed to contradict what he continuously pitched to our team about unity, about sticking together and protecting one another. In the end, Buddy tried to take the blame himself, but that noble attempt was unacceptable to Coach Woods.

To his death, Tony was tormented by the betrayal and embarrassment he was forced to endure. In the mind of a guy as prideful and hard-wired as Tony, there was nothing worse than for someone to deliberately, selfishly fabricate a lie at his expense. No one loved Hartselle more than Tony, and no one was let down as much as Tony when he, along with Buddy, Jonathan, Eric, and Fred, were falsely convicted of a non-existent rule, shamed by the media, forced to sit in after school detention, required to buy a ticket to the game; to sit in the stands for thousands to behold; to then be branded with a spiteful stigma to carry for the rest of their lives.

> Missing from the action for Hartselle were Quarterback Johnny Burks and Runningback Steve Barnett. Both received injuries in the Emma Sansom game. Five players were disciplined for violating the team's curfew earlier in the week and were not allowed to play. They were Buddy McDaniel, Eric Caldwell, Tony Woodruff, Fred Chatman and Jonathan Anders.

Hartselle, 1973

"Johnny," my mother sang from the bottom of the stairs, "it's time for breakfast, and don't you want to know what surprise your father has for you?"

Curiosity caught my attention, along with the aroma of sizzling, hickory-smoked bacon. My stomach started to beg and I kicked the covers off the bed and sailed down the stairs.

"Are you ready to go?" Dad asked as he sipped his early morning coffee.

"Yes sir," I responded. "Where's Terry?"

"Terry? You mean Terrell, don't you?" my father responded with a chuckle. "He got up with the roosters this morning and is already outside."

Restless with excitement, Terrell barreled in from the carport demanding that I hurry up so that we could leave and find the surprise my father had offered the day before. I finished my eggs and grits with a glass of milk and ran upstairs to get dressed. After driving past several downtown buildings and through a couple of intersections, Dad turned into an Otasco department-store parking lot. We got out of the

9 The good times, with our dog, Ringo.

car, walked past the automobile service area and entered the store. My eyes opened wide with anticipation when my father stopped in front of the new bicycles.

"Do y'all see one you like?" he asked.

"Yes, sir," I responded as I stood in front of the bikes grinning ear to ear.

I kept thinking to myself how awesome each one looked as they shined in the morning sun. I walked up and down the aisles in a meticulous survey before I ultimately chose a green banana seat bike with chrome fenders. Terrell picked a blue three-speed, and I remember Dad having to help him climb aboard. Once we learned how to ride, we spent the entire summer touring the neighborhood on our new two-wheelers. Terrell and I did not go anywhere without our bicycles; we rode double, backward, played chase, chicken, and even rode in bike-a-thons for cancer research.

On one particular morning, my daredevil biker-ways got me injured. I was coasting along the edge of a nearby street not paying attention when my front tire dropped into a pothole. The jolt caused my tire to twist and strike the curb. I lost my balance and flipped head first over the front handlebars and rolled down a hill into a concrete drainage ditch. I got up, bawling in pain, and chewed myself out for making such a stupid mistake. Mom pitched a fit when I walked in the backdoor with my blood-splattered scratches, but what made the accident worse was her decision to cancel our plans to go swimming at the country club that afternoon. I begged and pleaded with her until she finally caved and allowed us to go.

As I grew up, there was a community of boys who became my consistent playmates, but none more so than my friend Jay Halford. He had jet-black hair and kept a dark tan most of the year. Jay was small and bony and a little temperamental which made it hilarious to see him get his dander up. Whenever he was pushed over the brink, his policy was to fight first and debate later. Jay fought like a kamikaze jet pilot and closed his eyes and swung wildly as he attacked. Like a rampaging bull, he continued to swing until he either connected with his opponent or stammered out of control to the ground.

Jay and I, along with the rest of the kids in our neighborhood, massed in the streets each day as soon as we arrived home from school. The rhythm of the seasons determined what type of activity would be on the day's agenda. During the summer months, we played a form of baseball called wiffleball that used plastic bats and plastic balls, once the trees began to shed their leaves we changed to football, and by winter we were playing basketball in our driveways. Amongst my friends, you had to be competitive and unafraid if you dared to play. I was a scrawny kid with a feisty attitude who had two of the quickest

10 me, Jay, and Terrell enjoying some television

feet in the neighborhood and had proven my worth in our competitions. On the other hand, Terrell demonstrated no talent nor proclivity for sports. He was small with little aggressive tendencies and was easily swallowed by his larger and more hostile opponents. Many times after our athletic battles he walked home bloodied and bruised, and on one occasion he had even chipped a tooth. Obviously, his glass eye was a huge hindrance, and Mom and Dad worried about his abilities, or lack thereof, especially the day he was beaten up by Big Red.

As the name suggests, Big Red was redheaded and a little overweight. His chubby face was creamy white with an outcrop of reddish peach fuzz forming sideburns along his puffy cheeks. He rarely participated in our seasonal sporting events, so when he appeared one Sunday afternoon late in the fall while we were playing football, we all were a little caught off guard.

"Hey, Big Red, you here to play?" Jay sarcastically asked.

"Nah, I've got to take care of something," he growled.

With blood-red lips drawn tight to his teeth, he stopped in front of my brother, poked his finger into Terrell's chest, and exclaimed, "You threw confetti on my yard last night?"

"No, I didn't," my brother defiantly replied as the throng of spectators stepped back in unison.

I thought for a moment and remembered seeing Big Red's yard earlier that morning as Terrell and I walked to church. I chuckled to myself when I saw thousands of white plastic beads, the type found in a bean bag chair, coating his yard. But that was nothing unusual to see as all of us neighborhood kids were constantly pulling pranks on one another.

"You're a dadgum liar. I know you did it," Big Red spat.

"I wasn't anywhere near your house last night," Terrell promised.

"You're a liar," Big Red shouted as he shoved his smaller opponent in the chest with both hands.

Terrell stumbled to the ground and Big Red seized the opportunity to pounce on his prey. Terrell kicked his feet and hands with all of his might and frantically tried to block Big Red's fists. I turned and looked, and to my surprise, not one person was making any attempt to end the insanity.

"You're going to clean it up," Big Red screamed as he continued his assault.

Wanting to stop the melee, I scanned the surroundings. I spotted a basketball lying next to a tree and hustled over and picked it up. I ran toward Big Red and with a bolt of adrenalin, I threw the ball as hard as I could. When the ball left my hand, I screamed, "Big Red!"

In mid-swing, he stopped and turned his head toward me. Simultaneously, the ball struck him square in the nose. He cupped his hands over his face bellowing in agony and like a freshly cut tree, he fell to the ground. Terrell stood up and backed away. I sensed the disbelief in the air as all eyes turned to look at me.

Big Red rolled over to his knees and raised his head. Bleeding from both nostrils, his face and hands dripped with blood. Fear had shortened his breath, forcing his hands to quiver as he tried to wipe his face. He staggered to his feet and slowly began walking through the yard. Needless to say, my rank in the pecking order rose a little with that infamous throw. From then on, Terrell did not play much outside with the rest of us. My parents bought him a trumpet, and on most afternoons we could hear him blaring away from our upstairs porch.

Chapter 13

Football Fridays, Bradshaw, 1982

The following Monday everyone returned to practice, but the mood on the field was subdued as if a cold, icy wind had wisped all excitement and warmth away. Oftentimes we started practice with several aggressive tackling drills that seemed to perk everyone's spirits. But on this day, we were deep in the doldrums of a miserable season, and if you took a survey of the team, the blame would be pointed directly at one person: Coach Woods. It was hard to look him in the eye, his sarcasm and his actions had built a wall of distrust and discontent. As seniors, we were all about ready to belly-up like an old dead fish, especially when Double Lip turned in his pads earlier in the week.

I had spent two weeks without practicing, but my ankle was finally beginning to feel better. I was running close to full speed, but sometimes when I tried to make a sharp turn, I felt a blistering pain in my foot. I did not know if the coaches noticed, but every time I was asked how my ankle felt, I responded "perfect." I made it a point to soak my foot every day before and after practice and eagerly stood in line in the taping room to have my ankle wrapped. In front of us was a trip to Florence to play the Bradshaw Bruins and I knew Terrell would be at the game. I wanted him to see me directing the offense, not limping on the sideline like a battered little dog.

I entered the preparation for the Bradshaw game with a sense of vigor. For ten long days, I had stood and agonizingly watched my teammates from the sideline. I was now ready to get back into action and was not about to let a moment or opportunity slip away. When the first-team offense was called, I grabbed my helmet and ran to the huddle.

"You're on the second team," Coach Woods stated, his tone plain and restrained.

"The second team?" I asked.

"You heard me," he quipped, then stepped away to my replacement.

The dejection on my face was painfully obvious when I turned and walked to the sideline.

"Don't worry, Johnny. Don't let it get you down. He's just screwin' with your head," Buddy consoled.

"I don't get it. Can't he see that I'm ready to go?" I urged.

"Word from the wise . . . he's nuts, and I wouldn't bank on anything. He's shit on me, and you may be next."

I left the field house that day thinking about my future. *Was I going to be dumped so Coach Woods could get a younger quarterback ready for next year? Had he blamed me for the losses?*

"Get in," Terrell stated as he leaned across the console of his car and unlocked the passenger door.

We had just finished a late practice and I was on my way home when Terrell suddenly pulled up beside me. I swiveled my head and observed my surroundings before opening the door and sliding inside.

He slipped the car into gear and slowly maneuvered out of the parking lot.

"How long have you been here?" I asked.

"Don't worry. Daddy Ray's not going to find out."

Terrell reached for the glove box and opened the door and removed a zip-lock bag.

"What are you doing?" I demanded when I noticed a pack of rolling papers and several buds of marijuana inside the bag.

"You tryin' to get me kicked off the team? Are you nuts?" I demanded to know.

"Everything's cool. Don't worry, we're not going to get caught," he casually responded.

"It's for me. You don't have to take a toke," he instructed. "Hey man," he followed, "I'm not giving up on going to Mobile."

"Are we back to that? Can't you give it a break?" I urged.

"It's so simple. I'll do all of the work. All you gotta do is sign a sheet of paper. I'll take care of everything from there."

"What about our parents?" I pressed.

"They won't be involved. They'll never know. It'll be just between you and me. That's what makes it so easy," he assured. "Just get the report card for me," he implored.

"Look, I don't like this at all. You're going to screw things up. Nobody will understand this. You know how daddy is, he'll get pissed. Can you imagine what he'll do if he finds out?"

"Daddy Ray?" he bitterly attacked. "This isn't about him. Do you think I give a shit about hurting his feelings? I was sent away. They cut me off from my brother. My friends. Everyone I knew," he insisted.

"They were trying to get you some help. You were constantly causing trouble. Do you remember any of that?" I questioned.

Hartselle, 1976

Miscreant behavior; is it learned or is it inherited? When I think of my brother I seem to always go back in time and ponder that question.

It was the Spirit of '76, and it was to be a spectacular summer. The turmoil of the Vietnam conflict ended a year earlier and a new wave of patriotism swept the country as the Olympics and the Bicentennial celebration fueled a rebirth in national pride. Flags were waved with a renewed passion as citizens watched Presidential candidates Gerald Ford and Jimmy Carter promise to usher in a new age of American integrity. I was eleven years old and was saying goodbye to my brother. His reign of terror had come to an end.

"Come on, I dare you," Terrell whispered to me.

From our den, I looked through the darkened hallway toward the kitchen as my mother continued a conversation on the phone. I turned to him.

"No, I don't want to."

"Why not? Come on, don't be chicken," he insisted.

Part of mom's afternoon routine was to relax with a cup of tea while sitting at the kitchen table gossiping with friends on the telephone. The phone was mounted to the adjacent wall and just below the phone was a wicker basket where she kept her purse. Terrell dared me to sneak to the kitchen doorway and reach around the entrance and take my mother's purse from the basket. I refused his challenge to which he responded by taking the dare upon himself.

Like the Grinch slithering through Cindy Lou's house, Terrell slowly undulated along the hallway floor and methodically squirmed his way to the right side of the entrance. He positioned himself parallel against the wall that separated the hallway from the kitchen and curled his left arm around the doorway. He breathlessly retrieved my mother's purse and while kneeling on the floor, he pulled two twenty-dollar-bills from her wallet. With a taunting gesture, he waved the money at me then skillfully returned the purse back to the basket. Mom was totally clueless to my brother, the thief.

As the days passed, I started noticing changes in Terrell's behavior as he was becoming more daring and impulsive. I also began finding odd things in dresser drawers and bathroom cabinets. Oddities like instant suntan lotion, bags of candy, a slingshot, and a mysterious, small metal capsule that was labeled CO_2. Within days I learned the purpose of the container when he convinced me to ride my bike with him to one of our favorite romping grounds, a wooded area along McClanahan Street that served as our version of Sherwood Forest.

Remote, secluded and with a small creek passing through, the thicket of oak and pine trees provided the two of us hours of exploration. During one such visit, I tried crossing the creek using a fallen tree trunk. After a couple of steps, I slipped and fell three or four feet into the shallow water below. Lying on my back, I recall looking up and being mad as hell when I saw Terrell bowled over with laughter. I climbed to my feet and angrily stepped to the embankment, but before I could get my second foot on dry land, I lost my balance and fell back into the water. By this time, Terrell was on his knees rolling in a mad laugh, and as I sat up in the stream I could not help but start to giggle with him.

As we arrived, we applied the brakes and coasted down a slow grade to the entrance of the woods. Like Rooster Cogburn, I raised my leg and dismounted my green banana seat stallion and was ready to ramble in the wilderness. After taking a few steps through the undergrowth, I turned to Terrell and watched him lift a BB gun from a pile of decaying leaves.

"What's that?" I stopped and asked.

"What does it look like, stupid? Come on, let's go shoot something," he replied as he disappeared behind several low branches.

I shucked his comments and followed him along a thick, dark trail that wove its way through several wild shrubs. Eventually, the pathway led to a barbed-wire fence that opened to a meadow where several cows were grazing. Terrell pulled out a small metal container labeled CO_2 and inserted it into the gun.

"What are you doing?" I asked, curious about what I had just witnessed.

"What does it look like, moron?" he responded as he pointed the gun toward the pasture.

"You're not going to shoot the cows are you?" I demanded.

"Shut up and leave me alone."

Terrell pointed his weapon and began firing at the unwitting animals. At first, his shots were off and the pellets fell short of their mark. But he soon discovered the gravity factor and aimed a little higher.

"Quit," I ordered when one of the animals flinched.

Terrell turned to me to say, "Watch this! I'm going to hit one in the eye."

"No," I replied and reached for his gun.

He confronted my opposition and pushed me away, "Let go, dipstick, and get outta here."

I started to reply, but before I could say a word, Terrell shoved the gun in my chest. His push was not overly aggressive, but it got my attention.

"I said get outta here," he ordered while pointing the gun in my direction.

I was scared and instinctively dove at his waist to keep from being shot. He dodged my tackle and I tumbled into a thorny sticker bush. As soon as my hands hit the ground, I squealed like a panicked pig and scrambled from the razor-like spines. I gritted my teeth and clenched my fists, furious that he was getting the best of me. Terrell turned the gun toward me and pulled the trigger. The pellet barely grazed my arm but burned like the sting of a pissed off mud-dauber. I leapt to my feet and started to run away as fast as I could. Moments later, a second shot struck me right in the ass. I climbed on my bike and hustled home fuming over the fact that Terrell had shot me. I told him I was going to tell, but I chickened out by the time I got to our driveway and kept my mouth shut.

After being shot by his BB gun, I was becoming more and more aware of a mean streak in Terrell. He became aggressive, rebellious, and unafraid. I consciously started watching his activities and could not understand some of the decisions he was making. He seemed hell-bent to destroy everything around him and the pace of his criminal activities was quickening.

After school one day, just before the start of summer, Terrell and I rode our bikes to a downtown Seven-Eleven to buy a soft drink and candy bar. When we walked out of the store, Terrell pulled a wad of candy from his pocket.

I asked him, "Did you steal that?"

He simply looked at me and got on his bike for the ride back home. Within moments, the warning lights from a railroad crossing came on and we could hear a train approaching from the distance. We hustled across the tracks on Hickory Street, then pedaled to the right and up a slope to a point just above the tracks. Terrell who was leading the ride stopped and suggested that we watch the train. I got off of my bike and signaled the train's conductor to sound the whistle.

"You'd better duck," Terrell ordered from behind me.

I turned to him and in his hands were several large rocks that he immediately began throwing at the train. The sounds were loud as the rocks clanged against the metal freight cars.

"Just wait for the caboose. I'm going to nail it," he boasted.

I did not respond and stepped on my bike and zoomed away.

When I got home I sat in the kitchen with my mother for a few minutes before Terrell burst into the room from the carport. His breathing was strained and he was gasping loudly trying to catch his breath. He pulled a pitcher of Kool-Aid from the refrigerator and filled a tall glass, joining me at the table.

"Is someone knocking at the door?" my mother asked.

In unison, all three of us walked to the front of the house. Across the threshold of the door was a man standing in tan slacks and a collared shirt. Mom unlocked the door and greeted the gentleman with a smile and handshake.

"Ma'am, I'm an inspector with the railroad. Do you have a son wearing blue-jean shorts and a red t-shirt?"

Mom looked at Terrell then turned to the gentleman and responded, "Yes, I do. Is there a problem?"

"Does he have blonde hair?"

"Yes, he does. What's this all about?" she inquired.

"It was reported that a boy matching your son's description was throwing rocks at one of our trains. I responded to the call and followed your son to this address."

Snapping her head toward Terrell, her lips drew tight and her jaw muscles flexed. "Do you need to arrest him?" she asked.

"Well, one of our employees riding on the caboose claimed that your son was chasing the train and throwing rocks at him."

"My God, in heaven. I want the two of you to go to the den and wait for me," Mom instructed before stepping onto the porch to talk to the investigator.

I walked with Terrell to the den and watched as he sat emotionless on the couch. I have often asked myself if my brother ever understood the difference between right and wrong. Did he have a conscience? Was there ever a voice in his head arguing with him to think about what he was doing? Or, was he so caught up with the adrenalin rush of living on the edge that he never stopped to contemplate the consequences of his actions? Terrell never showed any signs of remorse once he was caught, and I sometimes believe he enjoyed trying to squirm his way out of trouble.

Directly across the street from our house was a rustic white bungalow owned by Bob and Pat Woodruff. The Woodruff's were casual friends of my parents and were invited to dinner on various occasions. Together the couple worked for an engineering firm in Huntsville until Bob was selected to serve as county engineer. On most nights, just after twilight, Bob's routine was to take his dog outside for a final trip to potty.

Early one evening, I was downstairs in the den watching the evening news with my father when the front doorbell rang. Most visitors typically came to our backdoor, so I decided to follow my father to see who was at the door.

"Ray, did you know your boy's upstairs shooting at me?" Bob nervously huffed from the doorway.

Dad gave him a funny look then asked, "He's doing what?"

"You've got a little Charles Whitman upstairs on your porch," he griped, "He's shooting at me and my dog."

"Charles Whitman?" Dad replied.

Charles Joseph Whitman was a former marine who, in the summer of 1966, shot and killed several unsuspecting victims while perched atop the University of Texas clock tower. From his sniper's nest high above the city of Austin, Whitman fired unimpeded for over ninety minutes before law enforcement officers ended his reign of terror. The tower stood 28 stories in height and before his rampage was over, 15 people were killed and another 33 were injured.

"He doesn't own a gun, how could he be shooting at you?" Dad wanted to know.

"I could see his silhouette through your upstairs porch and I screamed at him to stop, but he just kept shooting. He scared the bejesus outta me and shot a hole in one of my windows. You need to go up there and take that gun from him."

My father was dumbfounded at the story but raced upstairs to find Terrell standing in his room.

"Have you been shooting a gun from the porch?"

"No sir," Terrell countered.

"Don't you dare lie to me," my father blasted. "Bob Woodruff said you've been up here shooting at him. Where's the gun? Give it to me right now," he ordered.

Terrell tucked his head underneath his bed and removed a pellet gun and placed it in my father's hand.

"When did you get this?" Dad asked.

"It's not mine. Stump let me use it. It's his," Terrell clarified.

11 Our home, The Sherrill House aka Terrell's Sniper's Nest

"Stump. This is Stump's?" Dad quizzed.

Stump Norwood lived a couple of blocks from us and became one of Terrell's closest friends at school. His nickname said it all. He was short and stocky, just like the stump of a massive tree. His high octane personality enabled him to roam the social scene at school with ease, and Terrell tagged along as his shadow. The two of them were good buddies and shared a passion for rambling through the neighborhood.

"Why are you up here shooting at Bob?"

"I wasn't. I was shooting at some squirrels," Terrell explained.

"Squirrels? You can't see squirrels this time of day," Dad followed. "You and I are going to march over to Bob and you're going to apologize to him. And when we get back, I'm going to whip your little ass. First thing tomorrow morning, you're going to get this gun out of here and back to Stump."

A few years ago I stopped by to see Bob and Pat and they showed me the hole in the window.

That same summer Mom and Dad offered us a trip to Disney World as an incentive if Terrell could stop wetting the bed. His challenge was to go for two weeks, and to our amazement, his bedwetting immediately ceased and my parents were delighted that their offer was paying dividends. But like so many times before, Terrell was perpetrating another con. Within days, our house reeked of stale urine, and my parents confronted him about the odor. At first, he denied knowing anything, but mom began searching for the source of the stench and discovered his wet sheets hidden in a closet upstairs.

With the hope of helping Terrell's problematic behavior, mom and dad talked with a psychologist in Decatur and took him every Saturday morning for counseling. For two years Terrell visited with the counselors at the treatment center, but in the end, his progress was limited at best. At thirteen years of age, he continued to wet the bed and his behavior was as devious as ever.

One evening I was walking down the steps from my bedroom to get a drink of water and heard my father's voice from the den. I stopped and listened as he voiced his frustrations and discussed a plan to either send Terrell to a juvenile home or a military school.

"That doctor in Decatur is useless. Hell, Marie, he's out of control."

"I don't know what to do, Ray," my mother countered.

"Tomorrow, I want you to go talk with Stump about that pellet gun. One of them shot out Rachel Oden's window, and I'll bet I know which one did," Dad replied.

Rachel Oden was a teacher at Hartselle Junior High and a good friend of my parents. She and her husband, Charlie, lived a couple of blocks from us and at various times she gossiped on the phone with my mother. Mrs. Oden kept tabs on Terrell at the junior high school and stayed in touch with mom concerning his behavior. Late in the school year, Terrell brought home an interesting report card, all As and one D. The D was in Mrs. Oden's math class and Terrell was subsequently grounded.

Not long after Terrell received his infamous report card, a neighbor saw him walking along the sidewalk with Stump just as the Oden's front windows were shattered. It was discovered that the windows were shot with a pellet gun and Stump and Terrell were the main suspects. Terrell confessed to being with Stump but denied shooting the gun and blamed his friend. My parents were determined to find the truth and Dad wanted my mother to start their investigation with Stump.

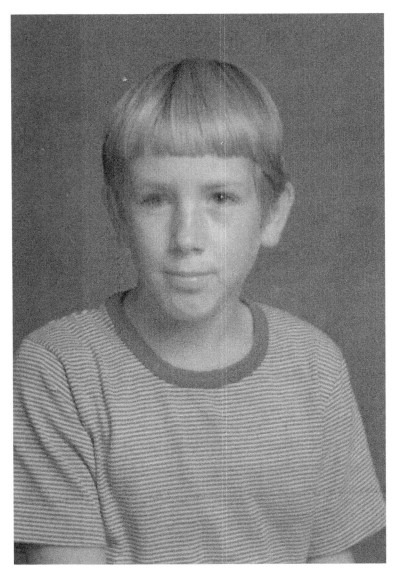

12 Terrell just before leaving for Florence

Chapter 14

Football Fridays, Bradshaw, 1982

After my conversation with Terrell, I went home and joined my mother in the den. I was thinking about his statements and decided to pick her for information. She was in the den sitting in a chair, crocheting an afghan blanket. Always the workaholic, Mom constantly kept her hands and mind busy. She appeared to be in a good mood, so I decided the time was right to quiz her for information.

"Mom, can I ask you a question?"

"Sure. What do you need to know?"

"Well, I was kind of wondering about the reasons why Terrell was sent away?"

My question stirred her brow and she immediately stopped her needlework. She looked at me and curiously asked, "Why do you want to know about him?"

"He was brought up today at school and I started thinking about him."

"Who brought him up?" she curiously asked.

"Buddy did. He asked a couple of questions about why Terrell was sent away and never came back," I nervously asked, anxious for answers.

"There were several reasons. You probably don't know about all the lies we were told, but your brother could tell some whoppers. He was so good at lying he could wiggle his way out of almost anything. But what really upset us was when we found out that he was sneaking into your father's bedroom in the middle of the night and stealing money from his wallet," she explained.

I remembered a lot of the things Terrell did, but I did not know he was caught sneaking into my father's room.

"Do you remember when Rachel Oden's windows were shot out?" she asked.

"Yes ma' am."

"Well, I went to see his friend Stump. I talked with him and found out more than I ever dreamed."

Stump told mom that Terrell walked around the neighborhood with lots of money and even flashed hundred-dollar-bills on occasions. He said Terrell bought guns and knives and liked to walk the neighborhood shooting at anything in sight. According to Mom, that's when they realized he was leading a secret life. Once they pieced his story together, they confronted him and demanded that he take them to where he was hiding his weapons and were shocked to find a small arsenal hidden behind our house.

"We gave him every second chance we possibly could, but Ray had had enough, and was afraid he might kill him. Remember the time he chased Terrell into the front yard?" she asked.

Hartselle, 1976

"Where's Terrell?" Dad asked from the doorway to the kitchen.

"He got sick over at Big Red's house," I replied.

"He's upstairs. I heard him walk in a little while ago," mom answered then turned and ordered me to go upstairs and tell him supper's ready.

Not wanting to leave my favorite meal of fried salmon and French fries, I shrunk my shoulders and reluctantly followed her command.

Terrell was curled in the fetal position in his bed when I instructed him to come downstairs for supper.

"I'm not hungry. I don't feel good," he mumbled, his face pale and wet.

"What's wrong?" I asked.

"My head hurts."

"Do you need Daddy?" I asked.

"No, no, it's not that bad," he countered.

"He sent me up here, so you'd better get up," I instructed.

"In a minute. Just leave me alone."

I left and scurried back to my delicious meal, not giving a flip about his headache.

"What's he doing?" Dad asked once I returned.

"He said he didn't feel good and would be down in a minute."

Dad sat his fork on his plate, moved his chair from the table and walked upstairs to see Terrell.

Sitting quietly with my mother at the dinner table, I heard bits and pieces of a tense conversation between Terrell and my father. I sat curiously as I finished my supper.

"He's been chewing tobacco," Dad stated when he returned to the kitchen.

"Chewing tobacco?" my mother puffed, "he's been chewing tobacco?"

"That's right. I told him to get his ass down here because he's not going to stove up in bed over something as stupid as tobacco."

Looking pasty and weak, Terrell quietly walked into the room and sat in a chair at the table.

"If you're not going to eat your fries, can I have them?" I joked.

"He'll eat every bite before he leaves this table," my mother answered. "I didn't spend an hour cooking for him not to eat anything."

"When did you start chewing?" Dad asked.

"I don't know," Terrell coolly remarked.

"Who gave you permission to use tobacco?"

"You did."

"Me? I did no such damn thing," Dad piped.

"You told me that tobacco was ok," Terrell complained.

My father's face blushed with blood, "You're a damn liar; I never said anything like that," he snapped as he reached across the table toward Terrell. Terrell lunged away from his grasp and fell out of his seat to the floor.

"You've lied the last time," Dad screamed as he stood and unbuckled his belt.

Terrell panicked to his feet and thrashed around the table toward the front of the house with my father an arm's length behind. Mom begged for them to stop and followed. The chase led through the front door and just as they reached the yard, Terrell was tackled to the grass.

For the third time in my life, I saw my brother pinned to the ground at the mercy of his attacker.

Terrell prayerfully pleaded for his life, "I'm sorry Daddy, I'm sorry!" as my father held his clenched fist in the air ready to strike.

"Don't, Ray, don't!" my mother begged.

Dad hesitated for a moment then turned and looked at my mother. Through a long, silent pause, he lowered his hand and rose to his feet. He then walked to the front porch steps and looked at mom and stated, "He's got to go, or I might kill him."

"Why was he sent to Florence?" I asked as mom continued to knit her blanket.

"It was either that or military school. We called our social worker and told her we needed help and it wasn't long until they called and mentioned the home in Florence. Our hope was that he would receive some serious counseling that might help him," she explained.

I understood her explanation, but the question that had continued to run through my mind was the reason why he was never allowed to return.

"Why didn't he ever get to come back?" I asked.

Mom thought for a moment before she responded, "I don't know if you remember this, but when Terrell was eleven I started taking him to see a psychiatrist in Decatur."

"Yeah, I remember that."

"When we pieced together what he was doing, we confronted Terrell. We made him show us everything that he had bought with the money he had stolen from Ray. There were guns, knives, matches, fireworks, cigarette lighters. We were stunned. Even after we took him to Florence, I found guns hidden in this house. I found one in the attic hidden under a stack of Christmas boxes."

"Why did he have all the guns?"

"That's what I went to see the psychiatrist about. I was bothered because we had spent so much money and Terrell had not gotten any better. As I was griping to the psychiatrist, I showed him a box of the guns, and knives I had found. All of a sudden the doctor interrupted me and began to apologize. He told me that he should have warned me sooner."

"Warned you about what?" I asked.

"The doctor told me the reason Terrell was buying guns was that he hated women."

"He hates who?" I quizzed.

"The doctor said that Terrell hated women and that was why he was collecting the guns and knives. He thought my life was in danger. He thought Terrell might use the guns on me. The doctor didn't think I was safe. Ray and I talked and believed we could save you, but decided it was best for everyone that Terrell remained in Florence."

It took a few moments to comprehend what she had explained, but in my mind the more I thought, the more it all started to make sense. I understood why my brother hated women, especially those who had control over his life.

Football Fridays, Bradshaw, 1982

When we walked out of the dressing room at Braly Stadium and began our pre-game warm-ups against Bradshaw, I was determined to show Coach Woods that my injury had healed and went through warm-ups as meticulously as possible. I desperately wanted to play because I knew somewhere floating around the stadium was Terrell. I stood on the sideline as close as possible to Coach Woods, hoping he might cave in to the pressure of my evil eye and put me in the ballgame. I'm pretty sure it was not my 'eye,' but halfway through the first quarter, I was back in action.

With less than two minutes left in the game, Bradshaw held a 21-14 lead. We were driving the ball when I took a snap from the center at the fifty-yard line and dropped three steps back from the line of scrimmage. I looked to my left and saw Eric who was running a slant pattern into the middle of the field just underneath a cornerback. I flicked a quick pass that he grabbed in full stride, his legs driving between two defenders toward the end zone. At the fifteen yard line, a Bradshaw defender grabbed his knees and as Eric fell to the ground the ball squirted loose. Instantly, a chaotic melee of pushing arms and diving bodies fought for possession of the ball. Coaches and players from both sidelines rushed to the field as the skirmish quickly intensified. Like everyone else, I ran to the tussle and stood watching as Coach Woods and the referees pulled players from the skirmish.

"Y'all are a bunch of pussies," a Bradshaw player screamed in my ear.

"Bull shit," I countered as I turned to him.

He pushed me in the chest and I instantly jumped toward him grabbing his facemask just before we both fell to the ground. I clawed at his chin strap in an attempt to remove his helmet so I could get to his big fat mouth. Unfortunately, the two of us were separated along with everyone else.

In the aftermath, the referees declared Eric had been tackled before the ball was fumbled and we were given possession of the ball at the seven-yard line.

With one minute left in the game, I called the play in the huddle, "Eleven counter-option."

We went to the line of scrimmage and I barked the cadence. I took the snap and pivoted left then right and faked a handoff to a running back. As I moved down the line of scrimmage, I focused on the defensive end. If he moved toward me, I would pitch the ball to the trailing halfback. The other option was for me to keep the ball if the end moved away from me. As I approached he stepped upfield which created a crease for me to turn and cross the line of scrimmage. I sprinted inside the opening in the defense and split two Bradshaw defenders as I crossed the goal line. With the extra point, we tied the score and sent the game to overtime.

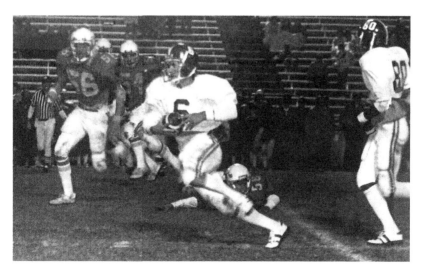

In overtime, we ultimately lost, but what came out of the game was more important. The brawl had somehow united us. Later that night, after we returned from Florence, Buddy, Tony, and some others joined in as we toasted our exploits with a couple of brews. The more we talked, the more we discovered our joy for playing football. We all agreed to commit ourselves toward finishing the season on our terms. Piss on Coach Woods, the football fathers, state rankings, piss on everything; it was time to play for our dreams. It was time to have fun.

Chapter 15

Football Fridays, Homecoming vs Athens, 1982

"Johnny, come down here," my father voiced from the bottom of the stairwell.

It was early Friday morning and I was getting ready for what I was hoping to be a fun day at school. But I knew immediately by the tone of his voice something was wrong. When I got to the bottom of the steps his breathing was rushed and his hands were nervously shaking his wallet.

"You stole my money?" he charged.

"I stole what?" I responded.

"You heard me. I had seven hundred dollars in my wallet yesterday and now it's gone."

"I don't know what you're talking about?" I claimed.

"You're a damn liar. There were seven one-hundred-dollar bills right here. Now, look. See. There's nothing," he exclaimed while pointing at his empty wallet.

I froze for a moment and felt sure he was confused. I did not know how I would be able to finesse my way out of this accusation, but I knew I was innocent.

"You say the money was where? Can I see your wallet?" I motioned.

He handed me his billfold and I asked him to show me exactly where in the wallet he placed the money. He pointed to a compartment and I searched the tiny crevices and found the bills hidden behind a tight flap of leather. I counted the money, and sure enough, seven one-hundred-dollar bills had been neatly folded and stashed away.

"Here's your money," I explained.

He said nothing, which was always the case. Ray Burks never apologized for anything, nor did he ever admit a mistake.

"I'm not Terrell. I'm not a thief," I replied looking sternly into his eyes.

That story pretty much described my relationship with my father during the Fall of 1982. He and I were distant and detached and had been for years. To me, the strain between the two of us began after Terrell was sent away. Within weeks, Dad suffered a massive heart attack, and even though it was never discussed between us, part of me believes he blamed Terrell and me for the stress that nearly caused his death. Before the heart attack, he and I shared a relationship and spent time together. In the driveway, he sometimes stood outside and watched me play basketball. Every fall he took me to the local Ford dealership and registered me for the Punt, Pass, and Kick competitions and then helped me practice. Many times on Saturday mornings, he took me with him to the nearby flea market where we watched the locals buy, sell, or trade merchandise. It was on these trade days that he introduced me to the southern tradition of drinking an RC Cola and eating a moon pie. But the most fun he and I shared occurred at the movie theater because my father loved to go to the movies, especially Disney movies with actor Dean Jones.

Dean Jones was a well respected and prolific actor from Decatur who belonged to an extended family of which several members lived in our neighborhood in Hartselle. He visited often and I remember riding with him in his car for family visits on a couple of occasions. In Decatur, Dad took me to either the Princess Movie Theater or The Gateway Theater to see some of Dean Jones' movies such as *Blackbeard's Ghost*, *That Darn Cat*, and *Herbie the Love Bug*. He also took me to see some classic films such as *Jaws*, *The Towering Inferno*, *Gone with the Wind*, and his all-time favorite, *Smokey and the Bandit*.

After his heart attack, those good times quickly ended. His personality became gloomy, and he stayed to himself. He became obsessed with horoscopes and read his daily. He also spent hours reading books about dreams and their subconscious meanings. My father was convinced he was near death and I remember visiting him in a mental health center on a couple of occasions after he claimed to be losing his mind.

At that time in my life, I had no idea what was happening to him, I was too young and too naive. But with age, I have learned the true nature and cause of his psychosis. My father had always been good with money. With the good fortune of the pharmacy, he had made investments in real estate, stocks, bonds, and had created a substantial financial portfolio. In 1977, at the age of fifty-five, he accepted an offer to buy his half of the pharmacy and retired to live off the income of his investments. Then suddenly, with no warning, he suffered the heart attack that brought his near-death experience. Being a registered pharmacist, Dad always believed medicine could cure any ailment, so he began treating himself for his self-diagnosed anxiety and depression. In our kitchen, he had long maintained his own little drugstore in one of the cabinets. Over time his self-medicating led to an intense addiction that lasted for years. As I think back, there were so many times that I remember him rumbling through his pills, then mixing his favorite cocktail of whiskey diluted with lemon juice. I never bothered to ask him what he had self-prescribed, I really didn't care, but I do recall him sleeping through the 1980s somewhere near Palookaville.

To this day, in my mind, I debate if it was better for him to have slept or to have been awake because when he was awake he appeared nervous and agitated, even panicky; like the morning he almost got us killed by a train.

"Get the hell out!" my father exclaimed as the whistle of the train roared towards us.

It was bitterly cold that day. I was fourteen years old and in the ninth grade. Dad was driving me to school when we approached the flashing lights of the Hickory Street railroad crossing. For me to arrive on time and not be tardy, we needed to cross the tracks before the train and make an immediate left turn onto Railroad Street. One by one the cars in front of us moved forward until it was our turn to cross. Dad and I looked to the left for the train which was about three to four hundred feet away. Always a punctual person who believed it was proper to show up for appointments early, I was a little surprised that morning to see him hesitate at the tracks when he knew the passing train would make me late for school.

I looked at the train and thought we had plenty of time and said, "Go on Daddy, you can beat it."

He turned and looked, then gradually pressed the gas pedal. Suddenly, there in the dead center of the tracks, in the middle of downtown school traffic, with the ear-piercing whistle of the train blaring at full throttle, the soon to be Titanic stalled. For a moment he and I looked at each other without uttering a sound, the two of us then turned and looked at the approaching train. My father's hands began shaking furiously, he screamed at me to get out as he grabbed the door handle and dove out of the car landing belly down on the tracks. As if his mind were flashing back to his World War II training days, he cupped his hands and arms to his chest and began rolling off the tracks before scrambling to his feet. I looked through the open door and could see the conductor's eyes getting closer and closer. I slid to the driver's seat and turned the key to the ignition. The car immediately cranked and I squealed off the tracks just before the train reached the intersection. Without saying a word, my father opened the passenger door, climbed in and I drove us to school.

Other than my early morning joust with Dad, the school day had flown by as we made our grand entrance into Tiger Stadium for our Homecoming game against number six ranked and undefeated Athens. Tiger Stadium had been built nearly a mile from Hartselle High School and tradition was for players to put their uniforms on at school, then load the buses for a short ride to the stadium. A police escort with emergency lights whirling and the piercing sounds of sirens booming indicated the gladiators were now entering the Coliseum.

Buddy and I were two of the captains for the game, and before we walked out for the coin toss, Buddy looked at me and said, "Johnny, this night is about having fun. Let's go have some!"

That's exactly what we did, especially Tony. Across the line of scrimmage from Coconut Head was Athen's best player, All-State defensive lineman, Mantille Stinnett. From the first snap of the game, Tony reveled in the competition between the two. On most nights, I made it a point to keep his chatter in check, but on this night I just listened and marveled. Coconut's mouth was at its best. The trash coming out of him was hilarious, and on a couple of occasions, I could not help but laugh because it was so funny.

Athens scored first, but we responded with a long touchdown drive that was set up with the play 413 - X streak. The design was for me to fake a handoff, then take two steps back and throw a long sideline pass to Eric. It worked perfectly and Eric caught the ball just before being tackled at the four-yard line. Two plays later I faked a handoff to my right then lunged into the endzone for the touchdown.

We took the lead for good on our next drive with the play 411 - X Post. With the snap, I reverse pivoted to fake a handoff through the middle of the line of scrimmage. I dropped straight back into the pocket and looked to my left to see Eric running through the middle of the field behind the defense. I threw a long pass that he caught in full stride and sprinted untouched into the end zone. With the lead and control of the offensive and defensive line of scrimmages, we shocked everyone that night with a 21-12 victory over the Golden Eagles. The

win improved our record to 2-4, and also afforded us a little redemption as Athens had defeated our rivals from Decatur 14-0 two weeks earlier.

After the celebratory bus ride back to the fieldhouse, I hustled home to get ready for the Homecoming dance and my date with Marilyn. I bathed as quickly as possible, then zipped up my slacks, buttoned my shirt, pulled my sweater over my head and headed to the Titanic.

In Hartselle on game days, it was a tradition for players to focus solely on football, which meant no girlfriends. A few hours of celibacy was the price to pay in order to prove your faithfulness to your teammates. There was to be no interaction of any kind beginning on Thursday night and concluding immediately after the game on Friday. Our game days were treated as solemn events and our behavior pretty much mirrored monks attending Mass. In fact, we wore our own version of a habit, grey slacks, dress shoes, and a collared crimson nylon shirt that was screened with the words Tiger Football on the right chest. Twenty-four hours of suppressing my libido had made me loopy with lust, and a fun Homecoming night with Marilyn was the exact remedy for my disposition.

Chapter 16

Football Fridays, Arab, 1982

Partying and drinking were constant in my hometown, and no matter what the occasion might be, there was always a celebration somewhere every Friday and Saturday night. Whether it was at a friend's house whose parents were away for the evening, a hastily called campout near the edge of the city, or cruising a lonesome gravel road weaving its way to nowhere, there was always a time and a place for a drunk fest. Earlier in the evening, we had shut out the Arab Knights 16-0, and Marilyn and I were headed to a party at a friend's house.

"Why did you change the station? I liked that song," Marilyn asked.

I was a little hesitant to answer because if I told the truth I knew the end result would not be good. "I don't know, I just did," I followed.

"Why are you suddenly so nervous," she wanted to know.

"What are you talking about? I'm not nervous." I replied.

"I can tell. Something is up with that song. You've done that twice," she finished.

"Twice? What do you mean?" I shot back.

"When that song comes on, you always change the station. And it's that song every time," she explained.

I felt stuck. She had caught on to something that I must have subliminally been doing. I wanted the conversation to end and remained silent.

"So, why do you change that song? You don't change any of their other songs."

"It's just a dopey song and they play it all the time." I countered.

"Come on, Johnny, I'm not stupid."

The song we were discussing was "Waiting For a Girl Like You" by the band Foreigner, and it just so happened to be a song I shared with a girl that I dated a year earlier. In the back of my head, I did not think it was a good idea for me to be listening to another girl's song while I was with Marilyn. I was a little unsure where this conversation was headed, so I continued to play dumb. Marilyn was having none of that and was determined to follow her instincts.

"Come on, you don't have to tell a fib," Marilyn pointed out.

Reluctantly I explained the situation with the song in hopes she would understand and we could move on with some fun.

Marilyn then asked, "Why did y'all break up?"

I thought for a moment and then explained, "I got a little antsy, I mean, I wanted to go hang out with Buddy and Tony. It got to the point where I was always with her. It got a little isolating and possessive."

With a serious look in her eye, she asked, "Is it that way with the two of us?"

"Of course not," I finished with a soothing smile.

The two of us arrived at the party which was a couple of blocks from Crestline Elementary School. The brick ranch style home belonged to a friend of ours who had graduated the previous year and whose parents were away for the weekend. I grabbed Marilyn's hand once we stepped through the front entrance, to meet a mass of beer drinking revelers who were smoking cigarettes and partying like it was 1999. I escorted Marilyn over to a cooler of beer and sifted through the floating beers, grabbing a couple of Budweisers for us to drink.

Marilyn and I had been dating for several weeks and over that time I had learned that she was not a heavy drinker. She was much like Buddy who was a well-known lightweight. Of all the drinkers in our school, and there were plenty, he had the least tolerance for alcohol. Buddy was notorious for being plastered after only drinking a couple of beers, then stumbling around the rest of the night. Many times we had to literally tote his tipsy butt around. This was the case one evening in New Orleans. A bunch of us were enjoying some cold beer in a bar on Canal Street when Buddy collapsed dead drunk after finishing a Long Island tea. Our waitress complained to us when he kept falling off his barstool and refused to sell us any more alcohol unless we sobered him up. Poochie and I lugged Buddy to the bathroom and helped him wash his face with cold water. We then walked him back to the bar and propped him against the table. Whenever we were ready to refresh our drinks we stood Buddy up and made him pay our tab as a reward for two good friends taking care of his drunken butt.

I was dumbfounded when I watched Marilyn turn her can of beer skywards and take a large swallow. I wasn't sure if that was good or bad, but I decided to follow her lead and matched her swallow for swallow. We mingled for a while, moving back and forth from the den to the carport. I continued to notice how much Marilyn was drinking and became concerned when she started slurring her speech. My biggest fear was for her to pull a Buddy and that I would have to take her home inebriated and unable to talk or walk.

"Marilyn, I think we need to go," I stressed with a stern look into her eyes.

"Why?" she asked. "We're having fun."

I offered her the ole 'it's late and I'm kind of tired' explanation, but that went nowhere and to my dismay, we stayed long enough for the full effects of the beer to take root in her brain. I looked around and saw my friend who was hosting the get-together and asked him if I could walk Marilyn to a back bedroom and let her sleep off some of the alcohol. He agreed and I held her close to me as we headed to a back bedroom. We walked in and I closed the door with my foot. I asked Marilyn to lay down for a few minutes, thinking ten to fifteen minutes of rest might help sober her up.

Moments later tears swelled in her eyes and she asked me, "Do you still have feelings for Lisa?"

I countered her question by telling her she was being silly and I had moved on from that relationship.

"Johnny," she mumbled, "I love you."

"I love you too, Marilyn," I replied.

I climbed into the bed and laid her head on my lap and stroked her hair as we rested for a little while.

After a period of time, I escorted Marilyn to the Titanic and opened the door for her to climb inside. From the party I made a couple of turns before pulling onto Nancy Ford Road and the drive to her house. Marilyn seemed a little better, but I was still nervous about whether or not she could pass a possible late-night interrogation by her parents.

"I think I'm going to throw up," Marilyn suddenly remarked.

"Oh God," I exclaimed while hastily rolling down the window. Stick your head out if you need to.

And with those instructions, Marilyn leaned her head out of the window and heaved the contents from her stomach. I looked in my rear-view mirror in hopes no one was driving close enough behind me to see what was happening and then quickly turned off of the highway and toward her house on Penn Road.

"Are you okay? How do you feel?" I asked.

"I feel so much better," she sighed. "I'm ready for bed."

I pulled into Marilyn's driveway just after midnight and walked her to the door. I noticed her parents' cars in the carport and asked, "What about your parents?"

"They went to Birmingham with friends," she explained. "They told me they wouldn't be back 'till around one o'clock."

Driving home, I was the happiest guy on planet Earth. Not only did we win our game that evened our record at 4-4, but the prettiest girl in the world told me that she loved me. And then to top the evening off, Marilyn would be fast asleep before her parents came home and noticed just how woozy their daughter was.

I woke up the following morning and lay in bed thinking about our upcoming opponent from Guntersville. For the community of Hartselle, it was to be the most anticipated game of the year, and for several reasons. The fact that the winner would lock up the area championship and a spot in the state playoffs was an obvious factor. But the elephant in the room was the imminent return of former coach Bucky Pitts who left Hartselle our freshman year to become head coach of the Guntersville Wildcats.

In his three year tenure at his new school, Coach Pitts had built the once fledgling Wildcats into a playoff contender and it had been reported to us that Guntersville was loaded with the best football talent the city had produced in years. At the start of the week, the media hyped the game as a battle of two talented football teams trying to make the playoffs, but by game day it was portrayed as a clash between coaches, the mentor versus the pupil.

Coach Woods had followed Bucky Pitts from the hills of east Tennessee to Hartselle in 1969. Their relationship lasted ten years and when the Guntersville position was offered, Coach Pitts asked his number one assistant to go with him. Initially, Coach Woods accepted, but the football fathers had other plans. Within days of Coach Pitts' departure, the pupil, the assistant coach who had agreed to follow his mentor, accepted the position as head coach of the Tigers. With his successes and failures came the usual comparisons to his mentor. Coach Woods used Bucky Pitts' offensive and defensive playbooks, and his critics were quick to mention that during his first two seasons he won with players that, at some point in time, had been coached by Bucky Pitts. The irony of the situation was the notion that it would be our senior class, the gutless wonders who were winless as freshmen, that would have to validate his abilities as a football coach.

After my musings of the upcoming game, I got out of bed and walked downstairs to the kitchen for my usual breakfast of toasted Pop-Tarts. I poured a cold glass of milk and sat down at the kitchen table with my nutritious meal. I was looking through the kitchen window when I saw my father walking through the carport with what appeared to be a hammer. I followed him with my eyes and then leaned forward when I saw some type of debris on the side of my car. I squinted my eyes to focus more clearly and quivered with angst when I realized Marilyn's puke from the night before had coated the passenger side of the Titanic from top to bottom. I thought holy hell if dad sees that puke, my life is over. I jumped to my feet and sprinted to the back door. I quietly turned the knob and pushed the storm door slowly open to see if Dad was anywhere near. With the coast being clear, I hustled to the car and turned the key to the ignition. I always left the car unlocked and the keys inside, hoping by chance someone would steal the car, but to my dismay that never happened. I backed the car from the carport to the driveway turnaround, making sure the throw-up side was facing away from the house. I ran to the kitchen and got a rag and some dishwashing detergent and went outside just as Dad approached me and asked what I was doing.

"I'm going to wash the Titanic," I confidently responded.

"Good," he replied with a hint of approval in his voice.

I breathed a sigh of relief as he turned and walked away. I made sure to give the green machine a nice bath and made sure every spatter of barf was cleaned from the car and no evidence was left behind.

Chapter 17

Football Fridays, Guntersville, 1982

Football's Split-Back Veer offense was invented in 1965 by the University of Houston football coach, Bill Yeoman. The strategy of the offense is to allow the quarterback to choose one of three options during the execution of a play. The triple-option, as it is widely known, allows the quarterback to either give the ball to a running back, keep the ball and run with it, or pitch the ball to a trailing running back. Decision making, timing, and the proper delivery of the football by the quarterback all determine the success of the offense. In its simplicity the concept of the option offense involves taking what the defense gives you, and it starts with the first option, does the quarterback give the ball or does he keep the ball?

"What determines if you give the ball?" Coach Woods demanded as I returned to the huddle after executing an inside Veer play.

It was near the end of our final practice in pads on Wednesday, two days before the area championship game against Guntersville. The weather was seemingly perfect for football, there was little humidity in the air and the temperature had hovered in the mid-60s all week. The energy and excitement during the practice could be felt as everyone knew there was something to prove, not for Coach Woods, but for our senior class. We were just days away from seeing, for the first time ever, Bucky Pitts stand on the visitor sideline in Tiger Stadium.

"If there is a collision, pull the ball," I thoughtfully explained.

"Hell no. That's not the way I've taught it," Coach Woods belted.

Immediately in my mind, I thought *here we go again.*

"I've told you over and over—if the defensive tackle steps inside to pull the ball," he angrily barked. "Here we are in week nine and I still can't get you to execute a simple play the way that it's supposed to be run. Why do I waste my time? Collision? There doesn't have to be a collision. If he steps down in there, pull it!" he screamed directly into my facemask. "Get out. Get out of the huddle," he ordered.

I stepped behind the huddle and walked over to Coach Pouncey as Coach Woods called out the next play for the offense to run. Our eyes met and I could tell from his facial expression that he agreed with me, but I could also sense that he did not want to talk about anything until later.

Coach Woods soon called for the team to gather around him where he began laying out the routine for us to follow over the next forty-eight hours. I could have cared less what came out of his mouth, the only thing I cared about was what came out of Coach Pouncey's mouth. I had moved on from Coach Woods, I no longer trusted him, I was going to follow Coach Pouncey.

"I don't know what to tell you, Johnny," Coach Pouncy remarked while shaking his head sideways. He and I were walking toward the fieldhouse after the conclusion of practice. "I'm kinda confused too. We've always said give the ball unless there is a collision. Running backs can run through arm tackles, a collision is totally different," he finished.

"What do I do if he calls 13 Veer Friday night," I wanted to know.

"Run it exactly the way you've practiced to run it. Unless there's a collision, give it," he instructed.

I felt vindicated by Coach Pouncey and began to finally realize that Coach Woods simply did not like me, and that was fine. If Coach Pouncey could see what was happening, so could everyone else, and that was all that mattered. I told him thanks and hustled to the locker room to shower because I had a date with Marilyn and I wanted to know her reaction from something I had left with her the previous night.

For a long time I had wanted to tell Marilyn how important she had become to me, so I wrote her a note and taped it to a .38 Special album that I left with her. I asked her to listen to the song "Fantasy Girl" because I lacked the wherewithal to express my feelings in person. I was learning so much from her about being truthful with your thoughts, but I was having trouble voicing what I was reallythinking. For me, it was easier to verbalize what I was thinking through the lyrics of a song, and I was definitely hoping Marilyn realized how serious I was with our relationship.

I splashed some Polo on my neck and wrists and headed from the locker room to the Titanic. I was surprised, yet thrilled to see Marilyn leaning against the driver's side door. She looked stunning in her tight jeans and blue chiffon blouse. I was lucky to have someone so beautiful, intelligent, and witty to spend time with.

"I love the song, Johnny. I had heard it before, but now I understand it and you're so sweet and thoughtful to be thinking of me while listening to that song," Marilyn reasoned.

I looked at her and smiled and said, "Well I'm lucky to have someone as wonderful as you in my life. You've made me so happy over the past few weeks and I don't know what the future holds, but right now I'd like to stay in this moment for as long as possible."

We fell into the Titanic and drove to McDonald's where we scrounged up all the money we had, which was enough to split a Big Mac and a coke. We laughed the entire evening and then I went home to dream about my *Fantasy Girl*.

It was a restless Thursday, but school finally gave way to late afternoon and we were in the midst of our final practice before the Guntersville game. Saturdays and Thursdays were the easiest days of the week during football season. From August till November, Saturdays were the only days away from the fieldhouse. Thursdays were skeleton practices in which we shed the pads and wore shorts and t-shirts. Our week's preparation ended at Tiger Stadium with a 30 to 45-minute walkthrough of the upcoming offensive, defensive, and kicking game strategies. Our final weekly practices were short, brief, and relaxed. That was the case for every Thursday practice I had been a part of until '311 Thursday.'

311 was a quick, play-action pass to the tight end. I had run the play hundreds of times because the design of the play worked perfectly for a team that utilized the option offense. It was simple in concept: after receiving the snap, I took a step with my left foot and pivoted around from the left side of the line of scrimmage back to right. As I faked a handoff to a running back, our tight end took a step away from the defensive end. He would then run straight upfield looking back toward me for the ball. With the play unfolding, I was to look for a gap between a linebacker and the free safety. If the gap was present, I could throw the ball. If the gap wasn't there I would continue the play by running toward the defensive end where I would either run the ball or option it to a running back.

I executed the play, but mistakenly threw the ball too far in front of the tight end who had no chance of catching the pass.

"What on earth was that?" Coach Woods fumed.

"My bad," I responded. "I led him too much."

"There's not a soul on that side of the field. Not one. And you can't complete a simple ten-yard pass? Run it again," he ordered.

The second time I was a little pissed and gunned the ball right at the receiver's hands. It was a perfect spiral that hit the tight end right in the chest, but he dropped it. I turned to return to the huddle but before I made two steps Coach Woods was in my face.

"You've got to be kidding me. You're so stupid that you'd throw a 90 mile per hour fastball to a guy ten yards away. Your job is to run the play the way you've been coached. You're back to freelancing. 'I'm not gonna do it the way I'm coached, I'm gonna run it my way'," he shouted with eyes squinted with disgust. "Run it a'damn'gen," he demanded.

What he actually meant was to run '311' three more times because that is how long it took for Coach Woods to stop yelling at me. I have never understood my passion for the game, and why I continued to play. Maybe it was the bond that I shared with my teammates. Perhaps it was the competition and the challenge to succeed. Then again, it might have been the girls. But I know one thing for sure, Coach Woods had absolutely no factor in why I played, but he would have been a huge factor if I had decided to quit.

After practice, I drove home to once again find Dad asleep on the couch. I walked by Mom who was in the kitchen gossiping on the phone. On the counter were juicy slices of ham with pinto beans and cornbread. Mom had a greasy delicious cornbread recipe, and she pressure-cooked her pinto beans with bacon slices and a ham bone for hours. The result was an awesome meal for a hungry appetite. I gobbled my dinner, then ran upstairs to play some tunes on my stereo.

As I was turning my stereo on, the phone rang, but I ignored it and thumbed my way through my record collection. I had a huge pile of albums and cassettes that I had acquired through the ever-popular Columbia House Record Club. To be a member the deal was simple; you would be sent several albums or tapes of your choosing for a penny if you agreed to purchase eight more at Record Club pricing. Every four weeks the club would mail you their collection list along with a predetermined Selection of the Month card. There was only one caveat, if you did not mail in those annoying Selection of the Month cards on time, they would automatically mail you the choice they had selected along with a bill. In my collection were staples like KISS, the Eagles, and Lynyrd Skynyrd, and with the age of MTV, I had branched out to some new wave bands like The Clash and A Flock of Seagulls. Also in my trove were some duds as a result of not mailing in that stupid Selection of the Month card.

A short while later above the decibels of my stereo, I could hear Mom telling me to pick up the phone. I grabbed the receiver and waited for the sound of the click indicating that she had hung up before I remarked, "Hello."

"What's up, man?" the voice asked.

"Who is this?" I inquired.

"Who do you think it is, stupid?" Terrell asked.

"Awe man, what do you want?"

"I'm at the telephone booth on Main Street. Come meet me over here," he instructed.

"I can't do that and you know it."

"Well you can drive down here," he made clear, "or I'm coming over there."

Backed into a corner, I felt it wise to do as he requested. I threw on some clothes and told Mom I was running over to Lyn's house for a minute.

I found Terrell at a parking lot across from the Western Auto and behind a gift shop known as Joe Roberts. It was dark and a little cool, but a couple of street lamps provided the light necessary for the two of us to see each other.

I forced a smile and asked, "Why are you here?" I scanned his eyes and told him I did not have much time to chat, "I've got to get home," I continued, "Look, Terrell, I think you need to . . ."

"For the last time, my name's not Terrell. It's Brian. Brian Dale Smith. I'm tired of you not calling me by my name."

"What's the big deal?" I questioned. "Hell, you've had so many names I can't keep up with all of them. Let's see, you've gone from Terry, to Terrell, to Stoney, and now to Brian. Jesus, look at how many names you've had. You're like a chameleon. Who am I talking to today?" I asked.

"Guess what your name is, dipshit?" he replied. "It's Roberts, Johnny Roberts! When will you understand that good ole Ray and Marie adopted you? They're paper parents, not real parents."

"Real parents? You sound so stupid when you say that. Do real parents put you in foster homes?" I quizzed.

"Come on, Johnny! I'm tired of not knowing who we are. How long do we have to live a secret? Five more years? Ten more years? Eternity?" he asked. "We've lived the lie long enough. I'm tired of having to put everyone's feelings before my own. It's not right, it's bullshit."

"I'm happy where I am. Damn, Terrell, you've got to stop running away every time some catastrophe happens," I explained. "It's like you want some type of new existence. You screw up, you create a new identity, a new personality, a new name. You think that's how you erase the past—your mistakes. Where did you come up with Stoney? What about Brian? I'll bet you got the name Dale from your buddy Dale Golden? Didn't you?" I argued, confident that I had figured him out.

"Kind of," he admitted.

Dale Golden became a friend of Terrell's while the two were in elementary school. Dale was popular among his classmates, especially the girls who liked his boyish good looks. He was viewed magnanimously by Terrell who liked to claim that Dale was his best friend. Terrell fancied the way Dale presented himself and even copied some of his mannerisms.

"You've moved from one family to the next so often that you don't know who you are. You went to Florence and tried to become Dale."

"No, I didn't," he responded.

"I think you did. If you're so happy, then why do you want to open our adoption records? I mean, why are we standing here arguing over names and records?"

We stared at each other for a moment until he replied with a slow sigh, "I don't know."

"Look, man, you're my brother, Terrell Burks. I don't think I'll ever be able to call you anything else. It doesn't matter to me if we have different parents or different names. What matters is that we try to stay together. There have been so many times that I wished you were still here with me. But that will never happen. Mom and Dad don't trust you."

"Why? I never did anything to them," he argued.

"What about the money? The lies? The guns? You forgot about all of that, didn't you?" I declared.

"I was just a kid. I was trying to impress my friends. Couldn't they realize that?" he asked.

"It was the guns more than anything. You really scared them with the guns. What were they for?" I wanted to know.

"I don't know. For fun I guess. I liked shooting things."

"You were shooting at people, not things. Do you remember a while back when you asked why you were never allowed to return home?"

"Yeah. Did they tell you?" he shot back.

"I talked with mom about it. She told me about your trips for counseling to Decatur. After you were sent away, she talked with your doctor about the guns and knives." I explained.

"What did he say?" Terrell asked.

"He told mom that you hated her. He said you hated women altogether. He said the guns were a sign that her life might be in danger."

"No way. He said that?" he argued.

"Hell yes he did, and that's why you weren't allowed to come home."

"That's such bull. I wonder how he came up with that. I can't remember anything we discussed about mom," he stated

"I think you're still mad at her, at Mobile. That's who you hate. The doctor got it wrong. It wasn't mom, it was her. That's what those addresses are about, that's why you want to go to Mobile. You want some type of revenge for what she did."

"No, I don't. I'm just curious. Don't you ever want to know who we are? It's got to run through your mind."

"My life is here. Mobile was a long time ago. Your life's in Florence. Sooner or later, you've got to let the past go. Let her go. Those people in Florence have got to care about you. They've given you a new life, a fresh start. Don't mess that up."

For some reason, I reached to hug him and could feel a sense of love between us as we embraced. It was the first time in forever that the two of us showed a sincere display of affection toward each other. I told him I had to go and that we would talk later. He wished me good luck and turned to walk away, and for some reason, I was feeling good about myself. Finally, he and I connected, or at least it felt that way.

Chapter 18

It started out like any other Friday. I woke myself up for school, then took my warm bath and grabbed a Pop-Tart on my way to the carport. The Senior Girls had neatly decorated the Titanic with paper streamers, balloons, and inside was a bag of Jolly Ranchers, Smarties, and other candies. I had all of my assignments ready for my teachers and was a happy little camper walking through the metal doors at Hartselle High School for the Guntersville game. As a team captain, I walked to the microphone and made an impassioned get-fired-up speech during the Pep Rally.

"Who do you think you are?" Coach Woods asked from behind his office desk later in the day.

"Sir?" I confusedly responded.

"I didn't know you were now so important that you are on a first-name basis with Coach Pitts," he coarsely replied.

I thought for a moment, then realized what he was bringing to my attention. During my get-fired-up speech, I made mention of the fact that Coach Pitts had left Hartselle and now he was returning, not as a friend, but a foe. I stated that Hartselle was not his homeanymore. Something to the effect of, "this is not Bucky Pitts' home, it is ours. And people have to protect their homes." Coach Woods latched ontothe comment and launched into a lecture about being disrespectful and that in using Bucky Pitts instead of Coach Pitts, I was being cocky and arrogant.

I felt a little hollow inside because that was not my intention, and once again my actions had been misunderstood. I took my schooling from Coach Woods and eagerly left the locker room to go home and get my head right for the game. Little did I know that the nastiest of arguments was only moments away.

It never failed, each afternoon when I arrived home and walked into the house I expected to see Dad lying on the couch in our den. However, on this day, he was awake and clearly agitated.

"Johnny, come in here," he called.

I walked slowly to the den, unsure of what to expect because he and I had not spoken much for weeks. Why all of a sudden would he want to talk to me?

I entered the doorway and said, "What's up?"

With a serious look on his face, he countered, "Stewart told me this afternoon that he saw Terrell riding in circles around the neighborhood yesterday. Do you know anything about that?" he asked.

"No sir," I replied.

"I bet you do. There's no way he drove over here without speaking to you. What are the two of you up to?" he questioned.

"Nothing. Nothing at all."

I didn't know Terrell had been driving around our neighborhood waiting on me. All of a sudden I was pissed. He drove around on purpose, he wanted someone to see him and Stewart Bennett happened to be that person. Stewart was an elementary school teacher at

Burleson, the school Terrell and I attended as youngsters. He and his father, Emmitt, lived together across the street from our house and the two of them were close friends with my parents. In fact, Stewart had been my 5th-grade teacher and I had a lot of respect for him.

"I'll bet he's been around here several times. Hasn't he?"

"He's popped in and out. He never tells me anything. He just shows up. I think he visits some of his old friends. Ask Stump or Dale. They would know more than me," I forced.

"I don't believe you. I've told you over and over to stay away from him and you continue to do exactly the opposite of what I say. I'm taking your car keys. I'm not allowing someone that I don't trust to drive my car," he finished.

I was ticked off and angry, "Why are you doing this? You act like I control what he does. He does what he wants to. Call Florence and tell his parents to stop him from coming to Hartselle. His parents need to be keeping tabs on him, not Mr. Bennett."

"I'm not calling anybody," he replied.

"Of all days, you pick today to bring this stupid crap up. The biggest game of the year and you're making this about Terrell," I reasoned.

"I don't care what day it is, I expect you to do as I tell you. I told you to stay away from him, but you lied and said you did," he lamented.

"That's right, you don't care about what day it is. You don't even realize that tonight is our last home game. Possibly the last time I play football in Hartselle. You don't care, you haven't even been to see one game this year. You won't even show up tonight. You'll be comatose on that stupid couch. You've never cared about anything I do," I cried.

He stood silent, then gritted his jaws tight, "Give me those keys."

"Fine. That's just fine. I'd rather walk than be held hostage by you. I don't control Terrell, I can't keep him out of Hartselle. It's not my fault he shows up. Why are you blaming me?" I demanded.

He said nothing, he just stood like a statue. That was my father's *modus operandi*, he got what he wanted, then removed himself both physically and emotionally. I reached in my pocket for the keys then slammed them in his hand. I stormed out of the den and went upstairs to my room. I grabbed some belongings and packed them into a duffle bag, then shuffled down the stairs and through the backdoor. I hustled around the side of the house to the front sidewalk and started walking toward the railroad tracks and the high school fieldhouse.

I have always been a hard-wired person who keeps my deepest thoughts stored within the recesses of my mind. As a foster child who moved from family to family, I was never around someone long enough to develop a close, meaningful relationship; the type of relationship where emotions are shared and trust is established. On the outside, I can give the impression that everything is fine, but sometimes the illusion cannot be concealed and on this particular day, the more steps I took along the railroad tracks toward the fieldhouse, the more my eyes watered. I railed to myself, *"Why me? What have I done to deserve this?"* My indignation was quickly replaced by rage, then resentment, then *kiss my ass.*

After entering the dressing room underneath the stadium bleachers for a few quiet moments, the quarterbacks and receivers jogged to the field to begin warming up. As I began throwing the football with another quarterback, my eyes were drawn to two men in bright red nylon jackets, leaning with their elbows against the fence that separated the stadium track from the field. They were staring right at me and no matter where I went, I could feel their eyes watching me. It was a strangeness I had never experienced before a game and I wasn't sure what to make of it.

Eventually, I turned to Coach Pouncey and pointed them out, "Coach, do you see those guys over there. They keep staring at me."

"They're college coaches, Johnny. They are here for the game. Forget about them," he finished.

I was both excited and relieved at Coach Pouncey's explanation; excited that they seemed to be interested in me, and relieved that they were not a couple of crazies trying to get into my head.

The timing, the sequencing, the steps; it was always the same meticulous movements, dance steps in every sense of the form. Each time we executed an option play, our movements had been coordinated into the most intricate of classical ballet performances. I never had to look for the running back, his steps and position had been coached to a precise location. I maintained eye contact with the defender. My job was to read, even predict, his actions as to whether I ran the ball or pitched the ball. Late in the first quarter, just before being tackled by a Guntersville defensive end, I pitched the ball with my left hand to Tucker Smith, a running back and fellow senior. Tucker was in perfect pitch position and caught the option and sprinted along the Hartselle sideline sixty-nine yards for the opening touchdown of the game. A beautiful performance that received a standing ovation from the audience. *Hartselle 7, Guntersville 0.*

On our next possession, we culminated a seventy-eight-yard drive with a short field goal and 10-0 lead. Later in the same quarter, Guntersville responded with a long drive that placed the ball inches from the goal line with seconds to go before halftime. On 3rd down, Poochie and his defensive comrades pushed forward across the line of scrimmage, causing Guntersville to lose control of the ball as the clock expired to zero. Following shutouts against the Cullman Bearcats and the Arab Knights, the Hartselle defense had kept opponents out of the endzone for a remarkable 10 consecutive quarters, and the home side of the stadium voiced their approval with a loud eruption of euphoria as we left the field for halftime.

As the coaches congregated in a tight mass of intense whispers, the players swapped hugs, high-fives and smiles in the locker room underneath the stadium. I took a quick drink and sat alone, leaning back against a concrete wall. After a long exhale, I closed my eyes and tried to relax my anxiousness. My body was flushed with epinephrine and my brain was trying to predict what was to happen in the moments to come. I had learned to calm myself and let the tidal wave of energy be absorbed by those around me because playing quarterback is unlike any other position in football. While the winds roar and the fire swirls, the quarterback has to have a somewhat placid effect on his teammates, one that calms them down during the chaos of competition. During the previous season, I was a defensive back, a position that required aggressiveness and a sense of nastiness. Halftimes were about maintaining an edge and staying jacked up with rage. As a quarterback you learn to keep your emotions in check, you take the good with the bad, and try to be calm in the middle of the panic.

"You've got to get your head around quicker," Coach Woods screamed as I approached the sideline. "We can't lay the ball on the damn ground," he raged immediately as our eyes locked. "Execute the damn play!"

On our opening drive of the second half, near our twenty-yard line, Coach Woods called a pass play that we had installed earlier in the week during practice. The play was a simple sprint out pass to a running back on the weak side of the formation. Simple in design, but flawed in one aspect; I had to reverse out which meant turning my back to the weakside defensive end. As soon as I turned around to find the running back, the defensive end had me in his grasp and the ball was knocked out of my hands at the nine-yard line. Three plays later Guntersville was in the endzone. *Hartselle 10, Guntersville 7.*

In football terms, to outflank an opponent means to have greater numbers on the side of the field where the play is being run. The concept is not complicated; always maintain more blockers than defenders. After the Guntersville kickoff, we had possession of the ball at the nineteen-yard line. I stood in the huddle and called the play given to me by Coach Woods, "17 Veer." When I walked to the line of scrimmage, I saw that Guntersville was running a 5-2 defense that had eagled down on the side where the play was designed to go, meaning the play had no chance because there were four defenders and we only had three blockers. While barking out the cadence, I audibled the play to the opposite side of the field where the Guntersville defense was outflanked by calling "13 Veer."

Once again the steps were honed and crisp, the movements rhythmic and in sequence, perfect practice creates a perfect play. Since the ninth grade, I had run "13 Veer" hundreds, possibly thousands, of times. I knew exactly what to expect, and on this night it was the same. The defensive tackle stepped inside as I inserted the ball into Tucker's chest. Collision! I pulled the ball and moved to phase two of the triple option. With my eyes in contact with the defensive end, he attacked my steps. With the ball in my hands, I turned my right thumb downwards as I extended my arm to pitch the ball to the running back. The Guntersville crowd roared as the ball flipped end over end to the ground. Our running back, Steve Barnett, had missed the audible and gone the wrong way.

Coach Woods was furious as I jogged to the sideline. His hands were slamming a manila folder against his thigh as he wailed in disgust, "What the hell are you doing? Why did you change the play? You're supposed to run the damn plays I call."

"They had eagled down, Coach. So I changed the play to the other side," I countered in the hope that he would understand my logic.

"At the 19-yard line we don't run the option," he screamed. "It's too damn dangerous!" he shot back. "Just run the play I call!" he railed in a loud tone spewing with contempt.

I stood silent next to Coach Pouncey who, sensing my frustration, grabbed me by the arm, "Next time just call a base play, something that doesn't involve a pitch."

"Yes sir," I nodded my head in agreement.

Moments later the incandescent lights of the scoreboard read *Hartselle 10, Guntersville 14.*

13 Coach Woods in action, 1982

It's amazing the absurdity of what people say and then turn around and do. After a stalled drive, Guntersville punted the ball to our 15-yard line. On first down, Coach Woods called the play '11 counter option.' Just as before, once the defensive end committed to tackling me, I optioned the ball once again to Steve. The timing was perfect and the ball flipped end over end, landing right in Steve's hands, but just before tucking the ball tight to his rib cage, the ball fell from his control and onto the field. The irony of Coach Woods calling an option play when the ball was inside our twenty-yard line might have been comical if the situation had not been so dire. Guntersville now had the ball, for the third time in the opening moments of the second half, right in front of our goal line.

Murphy's Law states that whatever can go wrong, will go wrong. It's a law that randomly reveals itself in sports, but when it does, it's usually at the most inopportune of times. In the third quarter against Guntersville, the law was on full display. How much screaming, cussing, exasperation, frustration and disgust can a player or a team take before they mentally succumb to the unrelenting pressure? The expectation of perfection, the endless badgering, the sneering, the criticism, the weight of it all; at some point in time we ask ourselves, is it all really worth the price I'm forced to pay? In the waning final moments of the third quarter against Guntersville, my teammates and I were confronted with that question. Should we continue to fight and solve the Murphy riddle?

As players, we learn practice is a key element in overcoming the Murphy conundrum. Day after day, time after time, we practice plays over and over with the understanding that perfection eliminates mistakes. But practice is mostly physical, which is the X in the $X + Y = Z$ equation that solves the Murphy dilemma. When adversity makes an appearance, in our minds we are forced to make a decision; panic and give in, or show some guts and do something. Thus the thoughts rampaging through our mind become the Y in solving the Murphy riddle. And when you play on a team, you learn you can see the Y just by looking into someone's eyes, their thoughts are visible and clear and they reveal everything.

Tony, Buddy, Poochie and the eighty other guys on our team were people that I had known and played sports with for years. Through the Park and Recreation leagues, we had all at some point been teammates or rivals. We had played together and against each other long enough to know how we would respond when Murphy's Law appeared in our midst. From the moment the ball fell to the ground late in the third quarter, there was no fear in anyone's eyes, there was no hesitation, there was no panic.

As soon as the Guntersville quarterback took the snap on first down and stepped to his right to hand the ball off, good 'ole Coconut Head immediately met the running back and slammed him to the ground for a one-yard loss. On second down, the Guntersville quarterback took the ball and sprinted to his right and flicked a short pass toward his tight end that was out of reach and incomplete. The play that followed produced one yard when the Guntersville quarterback was tackled at the 14-yard line. Facing 4th and 10, Coach Pitts had a challenging decision to make. Should he call out his field goal unit in hopes of pushing the scoring to 17-10, or should he keep the offense on the field and go for it on 4th down?

With 23 years of head coaching experience and state championships at two different schools, Coach Pitts had been in this situation before. He understood the line between playing it safe and sticking the nail in the coffin. There was a reason why in 1969, the football fathers crossed the Tennessee state line to hire a coach.

David Pitts knew how to win and seldom made the wrong decision. Never lacking confidence, and always trusting his instincts. Coach Pitts decided the time was right to stick it to his former team and chose to go for it on 4th down.

None of us were ever told why Coach Pitts resigned as football coach at Hartselle, we were only left with rumors. The money pockets in Guntersville were larger, the school system was better, the golf courses were greener; those were all ponged around the billiard halls and supper tables. But there was another rumor that echoed through the private conversations of the Football Fathers. It was the one rumor that resonated with my classmates, and it centered around an imminent drop in the talent level. Coach Pitts was there, he saw us as freshmen lose every game. I remember seeing him in the stadium watching us play, watching us lose. Maybe he thought the talent well in Hartselle was drying up, and maybe he thought 'get out while the gettin' is good.' Whatever motivation propelled him to Guntersville, we wanted desperately to lay that specific rumor to rest. Like me, Tony, Poochie, and Buddy reveled at the chance to prove the man wrong. Three long years of hearing the musings that we were part of the impetus for him to leave had constantly gnawed in our minds. It was like an itch you just can't seem to soothe. The answers to many questions would finally be made known in the events to come.

Grabbing the 4th down snap, the Guntersville quarterback took five steps back and settled into a semicircular ring of blockers. From the left side of the line of scrimmage, his tight end released toward the right side of the field, running a drag route just underneath the Hartselle linebackers. In a blip of a second, the ball sailed high and out of his reach.

It seemed as if a wave of nervous anxiety was released into the cool October air once the referee pointed 1st and 10 for Hartselle. With the ball back in our possession, in the huddle, I called the play '14 counter' to which Tucker took the handoff and plowed six yards through the Wildcat interior. On second down we ran '11 counter option' again, but this time Steve Barnett confidently grabbed the pitch and raced through the defense to the 45-yard line. A quick dive play netted an additional five yards and set the ball at midfield.

Guntersville was struggling to defend the rhythm and the execution of our plays. Their faces seemed a little confused and their steps a little unsure. Maybe Murphy's Law was paying their side of the field an unexpected late-night visit. Whatever the case may have been, we were gaining big chunks of yardage with each play.

Sometimes I ask myself, is there such a thing as a 'perfect play?" A play where all 11 guys do exactly what they are coached to do. If so, would a touchdown be the result on offense, and no gain be the result on defense? I lined up under center and recognized Guntersville was in a 3 deep coverage. I took the snap for the play '411 X - Post.' After faking a handoff to Tucker, I dropped back and looked for Eric to my left who was running a post route through the center of the Guntersville defense. I saw the cornerback and free safety were out of position and knew I could throw Eric open. I pronated my wrist and released the ball perfectly from the tip of my index finger. The ball spiraled tightly through the air as three uniformed bodies raced intensely across the field. Six hands reached high into the air for the ball, which landed stride for stride in Eric's grasp. Both Guntersville defenders had mistimed their jump and fell simultaneously to the ground as Eric caught the ball and raced untouched to the endzone.

There would be no more mistakes on this night, the Murphy quandary had been solved. In the fourth quarter, the Wildcats would cross the 50-yard line only once to see the drive end in a fumble when Tony plowed across the line and knocked the ball from the quarterback's grip. The final Guntersville possession ended at their 20-yard line as the scoreboard horn sounded, but there would be no congratulatory meeting between the two teams after the game. Both coaches had ordered their players to their respective locker rooms which obviously indicated some sort of animosity between the two. To their credit, I did watch them meet at midfield and share what appeared to be a resentful handshake.

In the aftermath, I grabbed my friends Tony, Chris and Buddy, and hugged their necks. We had proven the naysayers wrong. Years later, I remember hearing a comment in which Coach Pitts would make the statement: "I've done some dumb things in my life, but the dumbest was leaving Hartselle." On the bus ride back to the field house, I felt an enormous amount of pride swelling in my heart. We didn't succumb to the pressure, nor did we give in to the doubt. We simply proved to everyone else something we already knew about ourselves.

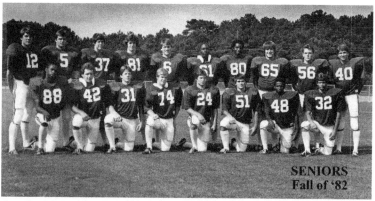

Bottom Row - left to right: Leo Williams, Jonathan Anders, Tucker Smith, Chris Keenum, Ray Halbrooks, Dale Robinson, Bennie Connor, Eddie Smith
Back Row - left to right: Scott McCarley, Buddy McDaniel, Joe Sanford, Lyn Long, Johnny Burks, Fred Chatman, Eric Caldwell, Tony Woodruff, Roger Bateman, Greg Caudal

Epilogue

I Know What You're Thinking

After winning the Area Championship, Buddy and I continued our
.38 Special air guitar concerts all the way to the State Semifinals where
we lost to the Oxford Yellow Jackets. A 7-7 halftime score ended in a
27-14 loss and concluded an 8-5 season. It was a remarkable
accomplishment, considering the constant drama and ever-changing
storyline we endured. For the seniors of that frustrating crusade to the
Semi-finals, there would be no individual postseason honors or awards,
no acknowledgments for anyone. And yet, Guntersville had two players
named to the All-State team and another one named to the state All-
Star Game. To our amazement, we were named Team of the Year by a
local radio station, and for a period of time the trophy stood in the
athletic display case at the school, but like everything else about the
Fall of '82, I'm sure it's been lost in time. I read a newspaper article
years later where a comment was made stating Coach Woods had done
his best coaching job ever in turning around our infamous season. I
laughed and thought to myself, *he didn't turn around anything, we
did*. And we did it, despite him.

Coach Woods never won an elusive football state championship,
but he did make one more championship game appearance. After
retiring from Hartselle, he accepted the head coaching job at
Morristown-Hamblen West High School in Tennessee. In 2003 his

team played for the title but lost. I tried to maintain a relationship with him after I graduated from college and began coaching high school football, but it would never happen. In fact, the last time I spoke with him he chewed me out. I had stopped by the fieldhouse one summer afternoon to let him know that I had decided to no longer coach football, that I just wanted to teach. He snapped a complaint to me that I was occupying a teaching position reserved for a football coach and that it was not right. I think he lost the idea that I wanted to be a teacher first and a coach second.

Leonard Edmunds 'Buddy' McDaniel owns a realty group in Gulf Shores, Alabama. He and I still maintain our friendship and talk often. He and his wife, Karen, have three children and enjoy a fantastic life at the beach.

Chris 'Poochie' Keenum graduated to what we all knew he would be, the best wildlife control expert on earth. He has two boys and lives just outside of Hartselle with his wife, Allison. He is self-employed and travels all over the state of Alabama helping people rid their homes, businesses and industries of unwanted vermin.

Tony 'Coconut Head' Woodruff graduated from the University of North Alabama with a degree in education. He taught high school history for a period of time before partnering with a friend to open a company specializing in industrial tires. We remained close friends and visited each other often until his death in 2019.

Marilyn Ridgeway and I continued to date for a period of time, but like most high school romances we eventually drifted apart. She graduated college and lives a good life with her family and friends.

My relationship with my father continued to deteriorate and by April of my senior year, he was chasing me out of our house with a pistol. I remember the incident like it was yesterday. He and my mother had gotten into a fight. Mom stormed out of the house and drove away, he turned and walked into the den where I was sitting and told me to leave. His eyes were glazed and his face was flushed. I sensed something was wrong and followed him into his bedroom. I watched from the doorway as he reached under his pillow where he kept a pistol.

He turned toward me with the pistol in his hand and I screamed, "No!" then turned and ran as fast as I could to the backdoor.

I sprinted through a row of shrubs lining our yard and hustled as fast as I could to the Halford's house across the street. Months went by before we were able to reconcile our relationship, and years went by before he owned up to his addiction. I'm still unsure if he ever stopped taking pills. We found hundreds in his safe after his death, but he did turn into a great father and friend. Dad died from lung cancer in 1999 and his last words spoken on this earth were, "I love Johnny."

Mom still maintains her happy spirit and lives near me. We visit constantly. Now in her 90s, she's a mother, grandmother, and great grandmother. Her passion remains Bridge and she plays with friends as much as possible. She and I have talked many times about our experiences during those tumultuous days and have learned to appreciate each other beyond measure. Thanks, mom, you've made my life so happy.

Did I ever look up the address? Yes. A couple of years after my daughter's birth, we joined a group of family friends in taking a trip to the Gulf coast. We rented a condominium near Mobile and I asked my friend Tom Oliver if he would drive down separately with me to find the residence. The postal address directed us to Rural Route 2 in the small town of Wilmer, Alabama. Tom and I arrived on a Saturday and pulled into the local post office to get directions for the route, but the office was closed. Not knowing anything about how the old Rural Route system worked, we found ourselves stuck at a gas station scratching our heads. Out of seemingly nowhere, I saw an old hardware store and thought to myself *I'll bet there's some old codger in there that knows something about rural routes.* Sure enough, I went inside and saw a nice looking elderly gentleman in the back of the store and asked him if he knew where Route 2 began. Without hesitation, he politely told me the exact location.

Tom and I quickly followed his directions and started winding up an inclining road. Suddenly, memories started to explode out from their hidden depths. I recognized the red dirt roads that exited from the route, the tall thin trees that sprang from every direction. My head was on a swivel and I remember being so excited as little fragments of my life seemed to be reappearing. Then in a spontaneous second my foot hit the brakes of my Jeep. I could feel the hair on the back of my neck stand on end, my heart pounded frantically with the intensity of a bass drum. There it was, I had not seen it in decades, but my mind instantly recognized it. The 'it' was a house that sat alone at the bottom of a sloping driveway about 30 to 40 feet from the road. The front yard was flat and empty, and the driveway was covered with a blend of sand and grass. Behind the house were tall oaks that were inter-mixed with dozens of Southern pines.

Desperately wanting to get closer, I backed my Jeep and drove down into the empty yard. I told Tom that my brother and I had once lived at this location. I opened the door and the smell was so distinct that it felt as if I was in a timewarp seeing myself, once again, in this yard, in the woods that were surrounding the two of us. I froze and stood silent and felt a hollow breath emptying my chest as another memory sprang forth. I suddenly remembered that this was the place where Terry lost his eye. The joy I was experiencing was instantly replaced with the burning, stinging sensation of regret.

After the nightmare that launched this odyssey, my daughter Abby was born, and she has been the greatest blessing I have ever received. My wife, Alana, and I have enjoyed a life filled with so many joys, but our beautiful daughter has been the greatest gift ever given to the two of us.

After the week of the Guntersville game, I never saw my brother again. Terry Roberts, Terrell Ray Burks, Stoney, Brian Dale Smith, had moved to Garland, Texas, and was installing security alarms when he died in a car wreck in February of 1985. I sometimes struggle trying to understand why I was the one who survived. Why was I the one given so much? Every time Terry 'Terrell' enters my mind I see a little boy desperately wanting to be accepted, someone who wanted to be liked by his friends. A boy who never seemed able to sculpt his own persona, his own identity. Unlike him, I could never see myself as anyone other than Johnny Burks. The last time we spoke, I just wanted him to know my name and know that I was not like him. I could not be another person, but I could still be his brother.

For what seems like forever, I have lived with a sense of loss, a sense of anger, a longing that things should have turned out better. Years ago, I stumbled across the phrase 'the randomness of fate' and I always keep pondering the notion that what happened to my brother could have happened to me. To my knowledge, he never located anyone in Mobile associated with our foster care or birth family, and I thank the Lord that I never gave him that address.

To my brother, this is for you . . . in my mind you will always be that little boy named Terry O'Neil Roberts, who was my protector during our darkest days. With God's Grace, we will see each other again.

14 one of the last photographs taken of my brother, 1985

And yes, the wicked dreams persist.

About the Author

Johnny Burks is an award-winning Nationally Board Certified Teacher. Mr. Burks is the author of several forensic science textbooks that are used in high schools throughout the United States. Mr. Burks is a graduate of Hartselle High School, Delta State University, and received his Master's degree from the University of Alabama. At Delta State, Johnny was a scholar-athlete and received Academic All-American honors. Presently, he lives with his wife Alana in historic downtown Huntsville, Alabama.

Made in the USA
Middletown, DE
26 November 2021